HORSE
LAUGHS

HORSE LAUGHS

by

Graham Sharpe

PRIDE
OF
PLACE

This Edition First Published in 1995
by
Pride of Place (UK) Ltd
Specialist Sports Publishers

10987654321

British Library Cataloguing in Publication Data.
A catalogue record for this book is available
from the British Library.

ISBN 1874645 450

Printed by
Redwood Books

PRIDE OF PLACE (UK) LTD
UNIT 22, CBTC,
EUXTON LANE, CHORLEY
LANCASHIRE PR7 6TE

DEDICATION

To all those who will regard
this collection as further,
if not conclusive, proof
that I'm a miserable old git

CONTENTS

PREFACE

I've never been able to tell jokes verbally, but I've always enjoyed hearing them — the less politically correct they are, the better!

Racing jokes are plentiful, but I have been unable to discover a compilation of them more recent than the 1930s — if you know of one I'd be interested to hear it.

Naturally, when you put together a compilation you have to impose your own selection policy whilst endeavouring to be as comprehensive as possible — what may be a hoary old gag with whiskers to you will be a brand new gem of innovation wit to the younger element, in particular who have never heard it before. Although that is not necessarily the case — as I believe I have illustrated within these pages.

Also, I am confident that this well intentioned volume could easily breed a follow-up collection. Particularly if everyone who reads it says: "I know a great story he's missed out."

If that is the case, feel free to let me know via the publisher and I will endeavour to include all contributions in any future publication.

The jokes, stories and quotes in Horse Laughs have been brought together from a multitude of sources. It is impossible to credit the originators of jokes since someone will invariably claim to have 'heard that one before' however new the teller believes it to be.

The difference between a joke, a humerous anecdote, a funny story or a witty comment is minimal and there are examples of all of them herein.

I hope you get a few smirks, smiles, grins and the occasional guffaw from Horse Laughs, but if you don't, just remember that it doesn't pay to take humour too seriously.

GRAHAM SHARPE
August 1995

JOCKEYS

Small men — tall stories

Quizzed before the 1992 Derby as to how long he could keep going as a jockey, Willie Carson commented: "As long as I'm still enjoying it, I'll carry on. I'm lucky because I have my athlete between my legs."

The jockey dismounted from the horse which had just been beaten because of his tendency to hang to the right in the final furlong.

"What can I do about it?" the trainer asked the jockey.

"Put a bit of lead in his left ear to balance him up," said the jockey.

"How can I do that?" asked the trainer.

"With a bloody shotgun."

The jockey was stood down from first place after barging his way through on the hot favourite to win the race.

After enduring a severe ticking off from the stewards he was dismissed from their presence having been disqualified from first place.

On his way out the jockey turned to the Senior Steward

and asked him: "What would you do if I called you a wanker?"

Replied the haughty Steward: "Most certainly I should suspend you for six weeks and fine you a considerable sum."

"And what would you do," asked the jockey "if I only thought you were a wanker?"

"Not much I COULD do about that, dear boy, one can't read minds, you know."

"In that case," said the jockey "I think you're a wanker." And he walked out.

☺   ☺   ☺

The race had been run on very heavy going — almost bottomless, in fact, and the winning jockey was telling the TV commentator: "On the way down to the start I spotted a jockey's cap on the ground, so I leaned down to pick it up.

"Just as I grabbed the top of the cap I heard a voice say 'Don't pull until I get my feet out of the stirrups.'"

☺   ☺   ☺

Jockey Richard Fox once offered to ride classic hope Risk Me in the 2,000 Guineas for trainer Paul Kelleway, only to receive the response: "I'll be up the graveyard with an effing shovel before you ride the horse."

☺   ☺   ☺

What's the difference between Lester Piggott and Michael Jackson? Lester Piggott can ride two, three, four and five year olds legally.

☺   ☺   ☺

Jockey Richard Fox again — he recalled being beaten one day in a race after which he told the trainer: "This horse needs six furlongs. He'll definitely win over that trip."

Retorted the owner: "Well, why didn't he win tonight? That WAS six furlongs."

☺   ☺   ☺

Former royal jump jockey Bill Smith told in *The Sporting Life* of the time when he and fellow rider Philip Blacker decided to have a drink after racing.

They met up with a trainer and one drink became two, then three: "When we were eventually leaving I said to Philip that I thought I was too drunk to drive my car. He replied that he was also too drunk to drive his.

"So we drove each other's. It seemed a good idea at the time."

☺   ☺   ☺

Peter Scudamore tells the tale of the World Jump Jockeys Challenge at which the jockey representing Italy could speak no English and the only interpreter to be found was an Italian waiter from the nearby town.

The waiter, something of a keen punter himself, was delighted to be privy to the information being relayed from trainer to jockey and, believing that the jockey's first runner was obviously expected to win, plunged a considerable proportion of his wages on the nose, only for the horse to finish well beaten.

However, when similarly optimistic instructions were delivered before the second race he went off with a fistful of lira to win his money back.

Once again the horse was beaten.

The Italian jockey was on the favourite in the third and final leg and the trainer told the waiter: "Tell him to track the leaders as he is a stayer with no acceleration."

The waiter, who was by now down to his last few bob, promptly said in Italian: "Drop him out last," and went off to back the second favourite.

☺   ☺   ☺

The young apprentice had arrived at Newmarket to begin working at a large stable but unfortunately they were temporarily unable to supply him with digs.

A passing jockey heard of the youngster's difficulties and suggested that he should try Lester Piggott who lived nearby in his large house.

The lad followed the directions he was given and eventually found Lester's impressive home. Nervously he rang the bell and after a few seconds there was Lester himself at the door.

"Er, M-m-ister P-p-iggott, can I stay here?" he stammered.

"Yes," answered Lester. "You CAN bloody well stay there."

And he slammed the door shut.

☺   ☺   ☺

The jockey was beaten on the hot favourite and his owner was not best pleased.

"Why the bloody hell didn't you go for that gap when it opened up?" he stormed.

"Well," replied the bemused jockey "the gap was going faster than we were."

☺   ☺   ☺

The hot favourite won the race in great style, but as the

14

jockey pulled his mount up he was accidentally unseated and crashed to the ground.

He was badly injured and rushed to hospital.

After collecting the huge winnings he had received courtesy of the jockey, a punter decided to ring the hospital and check on the jockey's state of health.

He was put through to the ward.

"Excuse me, sister, can you tell me how the jockey who was brought in earlier is getting on?"

"Shouldn't it be obvious?" said the sister.

"I beg your pardon?"

"Well, you said he's a jockey, didn't you?"

"Yes."

"Well, then, he's in a stable condition."

☺   ☺   ☺

The legendary Gordon Richards was about to receive his Knighthood. As the Monarch stepped forward to perform the ceremony, Richards declared: "I've always wanted to be known as the shortest knight of the year."

☺   ☺   ☺

In the days before photo finishes two horses came to the finishing line virtually together.

Although it was tight, jockey Brown was convinced he'd won, only for the judge to place him second.

In the next race, Brown came to the line well clear, stood up in the stirrups and shouted: "Oi, you bastard, its me again. Can you bloody well see me this time?"

☺   ☺   ☺

The jockey had just returned from his first meeting in France.

"How did you get on with the snails?" asked his friend.

"Well, I didn't eat any but I certainly rode a few."

☺   ☺   ☺

The Italian jockey hired to ride the British owner's horse in the Italian Derby had ridden a hopeless race and the horse was well beaten.

When the translator asked the owner if he wanted to say anything to the jockey the distraught owner shouted: "Tell him he's a c—t and he makes me scream," little believing that the message would be passed on.

To the owner's great surprise the translator actually began to pass on the message — but the jockey was smiling and nodding his head.

"Excuse me," said the owner to the translator. "What did you tell the jockey I said?"

"Just-a what you told-a me," replied the translator. "I tell-a him that-a his-a country make-a great ice-a cream."

☺   ☺   ☺

The apprentice jockey was being legged up for his first ride in public and he asked the trainer whether he was in with a shout of winning.

"Are you kidding? I've put a monkey on it and the wife's got a pony on it."

"Blimey — where am I going to sit then?"

☺   ☺   ☺

The French jockey who had ridden the Derby winner had been invited to attend a Grand Ball to celebrate and was asked to say a few words.

He spoke no English at all, but had asked a colleague to jot down a couple of appropriate lines for him which he could read out parrot fashion.

He duly arrived at the function with his notes, was introduced to great applause, stood up and, smiling nervously, began to speak: "Ladeez an' gennellmen, I em fuckin' glad to be 'ere wiz all you wankers....."

One of the jockeys about to take part in a two horse race was asked what he thought of his chances, and told the commentator: "I don't know, but whatever beats me will win."

The apprentice jockey was hauled up before the stewards to explain his riding of the hot favourite, which had failed to win.

"What instructions did the trainer give you?" demanded the chief steward.

"I was told to wait," said the jockey.

"Until when?" barked the steward.

"Until Saturday week at Newmarket, sir."

☺   ☺   ☺

"You'll get round safely enough on this one — it can jump houses," the trainer told the jockey just before the start of the race.

The horse fell at the first fence.

"What happened?" the trainer asked the jockey.

"He must have tripped over the bloody chimney."

☺   ☺   ☺

Four jockeys were killed in a car crash. Their wives arrived to identify the bodies.

Without hesitation one of the wives made straight for the fourth coffin and said, even before it had been opened, "That's my husband."

"How do you know?"
"He was never in the first three in his life — and it's too late for him to change now."

☺   ☺   ☺

As the horses jumped the last, the leading jockey suddenly found himself being pelted with tomatoes, apples, eggs, pickled onions, gherkins, even a bottle of champers.
At the stewards enquiry he was asked what had happened: "Couldn't you see?" he stormed, "I was bloody well hampered."

☺   ☺   ☺

Brough Scott to Walter Swinburn: "What are your immediate thoughts?"
Swinburn: "I don't have any immediate thoughts at the moment."

☺   ☺   ☺

It was once said of champion jockey, Fred Archer, that when he was a very young jockey he was found crying because he could not ride both winners in a dead-heat.

☺   ☺   ☺

Active in the 1950s, jockey Eph Smith once told a windy tale of a ride he had.
"I was told 'Cover him up until a furlong from home, then pull him wide and start farting right up to the line.'
"I thought the trainer must be as nutty as a fruitcake. How could anyone fart for a furlong with safety?
"So when it became dangerous to break wind any more I blew raspberries and the horse just held on.
"I shall expect a decent present — and what's more,

they'll be getting my laundry bill. Instructions like that could cause a nasty accident."

☺   ☺   ☺

Former Champion jump jockey, John Francome, had made an objection to the winner of a race at Worcester. The stewards sat and watched the film of the race half a dozen times, then one of them asked Francome whether he had any further comments to make.

Said Francome: "Yes sir — I've two actually. The first is that I'm bored with this film, and could you please put something different on — and, secondly, when will the usherette be bringing in the ice-cream and popcorn?"

Francome lost the objection.

☺   ☺   ☺

A week before he retired in November 1989, jockey Greville Starkey told *Sporting Life* readers that his ambition was: "To be chased out of a bedroom by a jealous husband on my 100th birthday."

☺   ☺   ☺

The *Sporting Life* report in April 1977 must have led to some ribald remarks to a certain jockey. Revealed the paper: "John Higgins fractured a bone in his left leg in a fall from Mrs Higgins at Edinburgh on Monday and will be out of action for a month."

☺   ☺   ☺

The two jockeys were comparing notes.

"I have to lose two pounds a day to ride at eight stone," said one.

"Just as well you do it, then," observed the other, "otherwise you'd weigh fifty stone by New Year's Eve."

☺   ☺   ☺

Former jockey Davy Jones, who was still riding winners at the age of 63, was asked what he had in mind when the time came to hang up his saddle: "I will ride racehorses, buy and sell racehorses, and, if I was starving, I would even eat racehorses..... but TRAIN racehorses — no."

☺   ☺   ☺

Lester Piggott was asked during a television interview what advice he would give to an aspiring young jockey: "I would tell him not to grow as big as I am."

☺   ☺   ☺

"Did you win?" Vincent O'Brien was heard to ask Lester Piggott after a very close finish to Deauville's Prix Kergorlay, in which Piggott on Reindeer had finished neck and neck with Precipice Wood.

"I don't know," said the taciturn jockey "I wasn't looking."

☺   ☺   ☺

Marcus Armytage recalled that former royal jockey, Dave Dick, was once in a Jermyn Street turkish bath sweating off some excess poundage when he overheard two professional punters in the steam room complaining about the ride he had given a Fontwell favourite recently. Instead of arguing the toss with the punters, Dick tied their door shut with some string, turned the heat up and departed, taking their trousers with him.

☺   ☺   ☺

Jockey, Simon McNeill, revealed his funniest moment in racing to the *Sporting Life* in March 1993:

"About 16 of us were called in by the stewards concerning a slow start at Newbury.

"I was stood at the back for my sins with John Francome and Steve Smith Eccles.

"Now Eccles had his hands cupped behind his back and spotting this Francome decided to move behind him.

"He promptly unzipped his breeches and then dropped a certain part of his anatomy right between the unfortunate feelers."

☺ ☺ ☺

In 1990 amateur rider, Peter Craggs, was one of the few jockeys riding to be adorned with a moustache.

"My only real problem," he told the *Racing Post* "is persuading my wife Nicky to wear a false one when she is schooling as this affects the horses' balance."

☺ ☺ ☺

Then there was the jockey who became the target of commentator Derek Thompson's dreaded and infamous instant interview upon returning to the Winners Enclosure immediately after a minor race.

Guffawing hugely the 'Big Fella' asked the jockey: "How do you feel about that?"

"Fine," replied the jockey. "By the way, can I say hello to my wife who's just given birth to our new son — and, by the way, we've named him after you."

"Hey, that's great — you've called your new son Derek."

"No," said the jockey "Wally."

☺ ☺ ☺

Two jockeys were headed for a race meeting at Southwell on its artificial surface.

One asked the other: "Do you prefer grass or fibresand?"

"I don't know — I've never smoked fibresand."

☺   ☺   ☺

Piggott and Eddery entered the gents together — Piggott made straight for the urinals and set about his business, but Eddery made a point of walking as far away as possible from the Maestro before unzipping.

"What's up with you then?" mumbled Piggott.

"Can't be too careful" replied Eddery, "Every time you spot a good thing you want to get your arse on it."

☺   ☺   ☺

After riding a disappointing runner, jockey Seamus O'Neill told the owner that his horse had made a noise at the end of the race. When the owner asked, "What sort of noise?" O'Neill said, "Eeore, ee-ore."

☺   ☺   ☺

The jockey had just arrived at the Pearly Gates where he asked St Peter for permission to enter.

"Sorry, we don't usually allow jockeys in — unless they've ridden classic winners or done something particularly out of the ordinary."

"Well," said the jockey, "I pulled up a 5/1 on favourite in a big race at Royal Ascot. When the crowd booed me I chucked my cap and whip at them and threatened to punch one of them. When the members jeered I spat at them and when the Chief Steward called me in for an enquiry I told him to go stuff himself."

"And when did this happen?" asked St Peter, intrigued.

"About thirty seconds ago."

☺   ☺   ☺

Asked once "What is your favourite race?" Lester Piggott told journalist Kurt Zechmeister, "A walk-over."

☺   ☺   ☺

The jockey was so convinced that his horse was a good thing that, strictly against the rules, he arranged to have a couple of hundred quid bet on it.

The horse made bad jumping mistakes all the way round the course, but was well clear coming to the last fence, but made an awful hash of it again and fell in a heap, despite desperate efforts by the jockey to keep him on his feet.

The jockey was steaming mad — he stormed up to the horse's trainer and told him, "You should do two things with that bastard horse — first retire him, then give him to your mother-in-law!"

☺   ☺   ☺

TV commentator, Derek Thompson, began an interview of a jockey by asking, "Have you always been small?"

☺   ☺   ☺

Spotted in the racing 'bible', the Sporting Life, this description of a Willie Carson victory; "Willie Carson, riding his 180th winner of the season, spent the last two furlongs looking over one shoulder, then another, even between his legs, but there was nothing there to worry him!"

☺   ☺   ☺

After French jockey Freddie Head had steered his Derby mount, Lyphard, on an extremely wide course around Tattenham Corner, jockey Geoff Lewis commented, "If Freddie rides at Epsom next year the gipsies will be asking for danger money."

☺   ☺   ☺

Having been jailed for certain disagreements with the Inland Revenue it may not have been wise for a fellow inmate to offer to take bets from Lester Piggott and adding "You won't have to pay tax."

☺   ☺   ☺

A jockey with the reputation for always finding whatever trouble was going during a race finally died.
The undertaker asked his wife what she wanted written on his headstone.
"Boxed in again" she said.

☺   ☺   ☺

Former Royal jockey Bill Smith, discussing the chances of a horse before his race at the Aintree Grand National meeting in 1992, commented: "This horse Randolph Place is a grand sort who would make a fine chaser, except that he doesn't like fences."

TRAINERS

A giggle of guv'nors

"For the last ten years all our horses have been bedded on newspaper — The Times," Luca Cumani revealed in November 1994, adding "if they win a big race they switch to the Financial Times — so they can read where to put their money."

☺   ☺   ☺

As trainer Tim Forster, a renowned pessimist, was once heard to remark: "If I hadn't already won three Grand Nationals I'd think I was fated never to win it."

☺   ☺   ☺

Then there was the trainer who prepared his charges on whisky, brandy and rum. "They may not be the best race-horses in the world, but they're certainly the bloody happiest," he was heard to comment.

☺   ☺   ☺

"Treat this horse gently," said the trainer to the jockey. "Give her an easy race and bring her in fourth or fifth."
The jockey duly carried out the instructions, with the horse finishing fourth of the twelve runners.
"Do you think you'll beat the three in front next time?"

asked the trainer.

"Undoubtedly," said the jockey "but I wouldn't be too sure about the eight behind."

☺   ☺   ☺

The trainer was bringing his top horse down from Scotland for a race at Newton Abbot in which the horse was due to land a big gambling coup.

He decided to drive down the day before, but got lost and decided he would have to find somewhere to spend the night before continuing the journey in the morning.

He pulled up at a farmhouse, explained the situation and asked whether he could stay and whether the farmer could put his runner, a mare, in his barn.

"Well, my stallion is kept in there and he's a right randy bugger," said the farmer.

"That's okay, I'll cover my mare with a sheet, she'll be all right."

Next morning the trainer went to fetch his mare, only to find the barn door hanging off its hinges. The stallion stood inside looking pleased with himself, but there was no sign of the mare.

The trainer set off down the nearest road, asking everyone he met: "Have you seen a horse covered with a white sheet anywhere around?"

No one had, until he came across an old boy leaning over a gate shaking his head and muttering: "Strangest thing I ever did see."

"Excuse me, sir, I'm looking for a horse of mine — she was covered in a white sheet and I think she may have come this way."

"No, young man," said the old boy "I ain't seen no 'orse in any old white sheet, but a while back I did see some 'orse come 'urtlin' past 'ere with an 'andkerchief shoved roight up its arse."

☺   ☺   ☺

The owner arrived at the stables unexpectedly to see his horse.

Unbeknown to the owner, the horse had fallen ill and the trainer had had it shot three weeks previously.

But he hadn't told the owner, hoping to be able to charge him for looking after the horse for as long as he could.

"Well, why on earth didn't you tell me?" demanded the owner, once he had discovered the truth.

"I saved you three weeks training fees as it was, do you mean to say you expected me to waste the cost of a first-class stamp as well?"

☺   ☺   ☺

The trainer was preparing his horse for the race and, as the jockey mounted, the trainer told him: "I've run out of patience with this bugger — if he doesn't produce the goods today I'm going to flog him to the local dairy to pull milk carts."

The race began and the horse was beginning to lose ground, so the jockey began to use his whip in encouragement.

Suddenly, the horse shouted to the jockey: "Go easy on me, mate — I've got to be up early in the morning."

☺   ☺   ☺

The jockey came in for a spare ride on a horse he'd never come across before.

"He's a bloody great jumper — the only thing is, you must remember as you come to the fences to call, 'one, two, UP' just as you want him to take off," instructed the trainer.

The race began, the runners came to the first fence, but, in all the hurly-burly of the race, the jockey forgot the 'one, two, UP' and his horse ploughed through the fence, almost crashing to the ground, and really shaking up the jockey.

"I'd better do what the trainer told me," he thought and, as they came to the next, he duly called, "one, two, UP" and the horse soared over the fence like a stag.

He didn't forget again, the horse jumped superbly and they won by twenty lengths.

Back in the winner's enclosure the jockey asked the trainer: "What's all that about then, the 'one, two, UP' business?"

"Oh, didn't I mention it?" said the trainer "the horse is blind."

☺ ☺ ☺

Two trainers in conversation: "I call my owners mush-rooms"

"Why's that?"

"Because I like to keep them in the dark and feed them tons of shit."

☺ ☺ ☺

The trainer had placed a huge ante-post bet on his big race runner and brought over a top Irish jockey to ride it. The horse was well beaten.

"Was the going too soft?" the trainer asked the jockey.

"T'be sure the going was no problem at all — it was the coming back which beat us."

☺ ☺ ☺

A crooked trainer sold off a useless old nag, which he

knew could never win a race, to a fellow trainer who he had always thought was a bit of a shrewdie.

Eventually, curiosity got the better of the first trainer and he asked the other: "How's that nag I sold you the other week?"

"Oh, the poor thing died the day after I bought him from you."

"I'm sorry to hear that," said the first.

"Not to worry," said the second. "I raffled him and sold over two thousand tickets at a fiver a go."

"But what did the winner say when he found out he'd won a dead horse?"

"Well, he wasn't too happy at first — but he calmed down when I gave him his fiver back."

A badly judged joke proved expensive for racehorse trainer, James Godding, in the mid-nineteenth century.

He looked after horses for the eccentric Earl of Glagow who, one evening, came to look around the stables.

Stopping at the box of a horse called Volunteer, Godding told the Earl: "It is a curious thing that the owner has never seen this colt, although he only lives a few miles from here."

"Indeed," replied the Earl "I should certainly have thought a gentleman would have come such a short journey to see such a good looking horse."

"Yes," replied Godding "but you see My Lord, the owner was born blind."

Far from appreciating this admittedly poor joke, the Earl promptly chased Godding all round his yard threatening to thrash him and immediately removed all his horses from the stable.

☺   ☺   ☺

Sir Piers Bengough, Her Majesty's representative at Ascot racecourse, always went out of his way to put visitors to the course at their ease.

One day he was introduced to a northern trainer who had never been to Ascot before.

"I'm Bengough," explained the Queen's man, discussing the afternoon's prospects with the trainer.

With racing over, the northern trainer was ready to take his leave. On his way out he encountered Sir Piers again.

"Ay oop, Ben lad — a reet grand day's racing its been — and give my regards to Mrs Gough, now."

☺   ☺   ☺

Commentator Derek Thompson was discussing a trainer's betting habits when he told viewers: "Mrs Knight certainly likes a nice little touch now and again."

☺   ☺   ☺

The bad tempered trainer had two horses running at the same meeting in different races.

Both were expected to win and he had booked the same jockey to ride both.

In the first race the trainer's horse ran very badly and, coming to the third fence, tragically collapsed and expired of a heart attack.

The jockey changed and came back to talk to the trainer who irascibly told him that he'd been 'jocked off' of the second mount and replaced by another jockey.

The race was run and the substitute jockey could only push the trainer's horse into seventh place.

On the way out of the track, the original jockey saw the trainer and said to him: "That second horse didn't run very

well did it. The other jockey didn't make much difference."
"No lad, he didn't ride it too well — but at least he didn't kill the bloody thing."

☺ ☺ ☺

The horse had finished the race lame and was being examined by his trainer as the vet walked past.
"This is odd," said the trainer. "This bugger is sometimes as sound as bell, then on other occasions he becomes lame for no apparent reason. What do you reckon?"
"I reckon you should wait until he's sound again," said the vet "and then sell the beast."

☺ ☺ ☺

Trainer-cum-comedian Richard Phillips recently divulged the reason that trainer Henry Cecil, a keen gardener, had received the honour of having a rose named after him.....
"Because it only has a gentle prick."

☺ ☺ ☺

The same source produced the following gag on Cheltenham's *Festival Radio* during the 1995 broadcast. Speaking in his best Derek Thompson voice, Phillips drawled: "And now to the picture puzzle. Yes, big fella, it's a picture of John Francome on top of Leslie Graham.
"And the answer is, yes big fella, Berude Not To."

☺ ☺ ☺

The following letter from trainer Michael Stoute appeared in the *Sporting Life* on February 9, 1995:
"I do believe the Barbadian who stole Willie Carson's wallet is a collector of rare items, and I am hopeful that it may one day soon be exhibited at the Barbados Museum — with all the white fivers still intact."

☺   ☺   ☺

"Averti switches off in his races," trainer Willie Muir told *The Guardian* in September 1993 "and has quietened down a lot since we first got him — when he was being broken he reared over on top of my wife Jeanette and broke her leg.

"Of course I did the wrong thing by rushing up and asking whether the horse was all right."

☺   ☺   ☺

Jockey turned trainer, Frankie Durr, was watching the progress of a runner at Huntingdon one day when the horse came round the final bend well clear only for it to slip and the jockey to fall off.

"I told him to find the best ground," remarked Durr. "But I didn't expect him to get off and look for it!"

☺   ☺   ☺

Another Frankie Durr story is recalled by fellow jock, Richard Fox, who recounted the tale of the time when, during the hustle and bustle of a finish he put out at arm to steady himself and inadvertently pushed Frankie, who lost an iron and almost came down.

"Sorry about that Frankie," Foxy told Durr "it was just a natural reaction."

"And so is this," replied Durr, knocking Fox flat.

☺   ☺   ☺

Trainer, Peter Easterby, was convinced his great old horse, dual Champion Hurdler, Sea Pigeon, was the most intelligent animal he'd ever looked after.

"He always turned up at the kitchen door at 1pm for his feed — never missed a day until one particular occasion when, come 1pm he hadn't arrived.

"I was getting a bit worried, but he finally turned up an hour later — turned out I'd forgotten to put my clock back that night."

☺ ☺ ☺

Upper class trainer Frank Butters was not one to regard the jockeys who rode his horses as trustworthy types as they did not come from the same social background as he did.

On one ocasion Butters was talking to an acquaintance about famous jockey Charlie Smirke, who was away fightiing in the Second World War.

"Have you heard the news Mr Butters?" asked the acquainatnce, "Charlie Smirke's been awarded the VC in Siciliy."

"Really, what for?" asked Butters, to be told, "For stopping a German tank."

"I'm not surprised" replied Butters, "When he was riding for me he would stop anything."

☺ ☺ ☺

TV viewers were mildly surprised at trainer Henry Cecil's anatomical knowledge of his racehorses when they heard him observe following the running of the 3.40 at Sandown on April 24, 192 about the winning horse Rudimentary, that "this time last year he was all arms and legs."

☺ ☺ ☺

The punter won so much money by backing the winner of a seller that he decided to buy it.

The horse, which had been specially prepared for this one race, suffered from bad legs, wall eyes, rotting teeth and a weak back.

The proud new owner took the horse along to his local

trainer, who took one look at it and asked him, "And what do you intend to do with that?"

"Well, I thought I'd race it."

"Judging by its appearance you'd have a great chance of beating it, too."

☺   ☺   ☺

Henry Cecil recalled the trainer who told his owner "I'm afraid the horse is still green," only to receive the reply, "He was brown the last time I saw him."

☺   ☺   ☺

Jeremy Tree was explaining to Lester Piggott that he had been invited to address the pupils at his old school, Eton. "I've to tell them all I know about racing — what shall I say?"

Lester thought briefly then advised, "Tell 'em you've got flu."

☺   ☺   ☺

The jockey and trainer were conferring after their 'good thing' had been turned over in the sprint race.

"Well, do you think he stays?" asked the trainer.

"Yes," said the jockey "too bloody long in the same place."

☺   ☺   ☺

The trainer was holding court in the winners' enclosure after his charge had bolted home in the big race.

"What are your plans for the horse?" asked a journalist.

"That," replied the trainer, "WAS the plan."

☺   ☺   ☺

The gambling trainer liked to butter his bread on both sides.

His biggest owner had a fancied horse entered for the big

race, the trainer had decided to 'pull' the horse.

He wrote to the owner, "My Lord, the horse is fit and raring to go. I am confident he cannot lose. Back him with all you can afford."

He wrote to his tame bookie, "Dear Joe, His Lanky Lordship will be at the course on Saturday to back his old nag. Lay him all he wants, it can't win."

The trainer put the letters in the wrong envelopes.

OWNERS

Paying the bills can be fun

The racehorse owner was finally forced to accept that his pride and joy was never likely to become a Derby winner, having trailed in last on ten consecutive occasions.

The trainer advised him that his last remaining option was to sell the horse at auction.

But the potential purchasers were less than enthused by the prospect of owning the horse, and the bidding stalled at just £10.

Raising his gavel the auctioneer turned to ask the owner: "Should I knock him down, sir?"

"Only as a last resort," said the owner "but sell him first if you can."

☺   ☺   ☺

"I call my trainer The Rhino" said one owner to another.
"Why's that?"
"Because he has a thick skin and charges a great deal."

☺   ☺   ☺

It was said of legendary professional backer Alex Bird that when he was plunging on a 'good thing' he would always go to bed alone — in case he talked in his sleep.

The excited racehorse owner rushed into his local betting shop and demanded to see the manager, telling him: "I've just dreamed that my horse will win next Saturday's Grand National."

"Oh yes?" said the bookie, "Then you'd better pinch yourself and wake up quickly — the old nag's a 500/1 shot. It couldn't win if it started now."

"No, it must have been a sign. I saw everything clearly, right down to the black armband the jockey was wearing.

"I saw them jump Becher's and I saw my horse go clear on the run-in to win by ten lengths. I MUST back him - put £1,000 on him for me."

"Well, its your money, if you want to chuck it away...." said the bookie.

Grand National Day came. The race went precisely as the owner had dreamed: his horse stormed away on the run-in to win by ten lengths. The jockey was even wearing the black armband.

Which explains why the owner never collected his winnings.

He had died the day before.

☺   ☺   ☺

The owner rang his stable and asked whether the trainer could make sure the yard would be spotlessly clean at 10.30 the next morning as he was bringing a friend along to look around the place.

Hoping to acquire more business, the trainer made sure his staff took extra care in cleaning the place up, and sure enough at 10.30 the owner and another man arrived.

The owner led his smartly dressed companion around, pointing out the different horses as he went.

The two stayed for half an hour then, thanking the trainer, they left.

Shortly after, as the trainer sat thinking to himself how pleasant it would be to gain another wealthy owner, his head lad knocked on the office door and asked him exactly when four of the best horses in the yard had changed hands and been bought by the owner who had been showing his friend around the yard that morning.

Puzzled, the trainer told the lad that the horses had not changed hands at all. "That's odd," said the lad "only the owner was telling his friend that all four of them were his, as well as the one he really does own."

The trainer forgot about the incident until later that evening when the owner rang him to ask about running plans for his horse.

"I've got him in a little race at Newton Abbot — he should win," said the trainer. "By the way, is that friend of yours going to buy a horse and let me train it for him?"

"Why?" said the owner. "What makes you think he'd do that?"

"Wasn't he a prospective owner, then?"

"Of course not," laughed the owner. "Why do you think I told him I owned those other four horses?"

"I've no idea."

"Well, he's my bank manager, and it's a hell of a lot easier to get a bigger overdraft when he thinks I've got five bloody good horses in training."

Actor and racehorse owner Wilfrid Hyde-White was making an unfortunate appearance in the bankruptcy court. During the course of his cross-examination the official receiver commented: "Mr Hyde-White, if you cannot tell us how you spent such a large sum in so short a time, perhaps you could tell us what will win the Gold Cup at Ascot this afternoon."

"Of course, dear fellow," replied the suave actor, naming the horse which did, in fact, go on to win the race. "But only have a small bet — we don't want to have to change places, do we?"

☺   ☺   ☺

The wealthy racehorse owner was always seen at the races with a glamorous but common looking female companion.

One day he arrived on his own to see one of his horses run.

"And where is your lady friend?" he was asked.

"I had to make up my mind whether to keep her or my horses and her entry fees were higher."

☺   ☺   ☺

The punter strode up to the bookie and asked him for a bet of £500 on the 10/1 outsider in the field of three runners.

The bookie took the bet, rubbed out the 10/1 and, to the punter's amazement, chalked up 12/1.

Back came the punter with another £500 which the bookie took, rubbed off 12/1 — and chalked up 14/1.

The punter returned again — another 'monkey' — but out went the odds to 16/1.

"Excuse me asking," said the punter "but why do you keep knocking the odds out every time I back that horse?"

"Well, now you've had your bets, I'll let you into a little secret. I happen to know that horse can't win. You see, I own it."

"Oh," said the punter. "This is going to be a bloody funny race then — I own the other two."

☺   ☺   ☺

Three bookies gathered round the grave of a recently deceased racegoer who had been a keen punter.

The first bookie, conscience stricken after the bereavement, looked down at the coffin and said: "He'd just backed a winner for twenty quid with me." And he dropped four fivers into the grave.

The second bookie looked down and said: "I'd just laid him four fivers about a winner, too." And he put two tenners on to the coffin.

The third bookie said: "He must have been on a winning streak, I owed him a score, too." And he took out his cheque book, wrote out a cheque for £60, dropped it into the grave and pocketed the £40 cash.

☺   ☺   ☺

"When a jumper I had wouldn't take a fence, the trainer seriously told me the horse would need psychiatric treatment. I knew that was enough and I got out."

......Showbiz tycoon and owner Lord Bernard Delfont.

☺   ☺   ☺

In 1878 eccentric owner Caroline, the Duchess of Montrose, was aggrieved at the way her horses were receiving too much weight from the handicapper.

Upon meeting the rather overweight handicapper, Major Egerton, she told him: "Major Egerton, I see from the way you handicap my horses that you are desirous of riding them yourself.

"I only intend to say that on no account will your wish be gratified."

Tony Hill, owner of Ann Hill, winner of a Lingfield race in June 1993, was asked why he'd named the horse after his wife: "Their back ends are similar."

☺   ☺   ☺

"There is nothing more expensive than owning horses, unless it is having relations who do."
.....Former Prime Minister Sir Alec Douglas-Home.

☺   ☺   ☺

The lady owner was not best pleased when, after being told to go easy on her horse when all chance of victory was gone, observed him thrashing the horse even though success was impossible.
When the jockey returned, the owner confronted him with the words: "I gave you a horse — you've given me back a bloody zebra."

☺   ☺   ☺

"He's done everything I've asked him at home," the trainer told the expectant owner shortly before the off.
"Excellent," replied the owner "and have you asked him to win this afternoon?"

☺   ☺   ☺

Jockey and journalist, Marcus Armytage, told this tale:-
The Newmarket trainer was well known for equipping his stables with a stereo system over which he played rock music to the inmates.
One of the trainer's owners was the type who quibbled over every item on his monthly bill.
The owner's horse had been injured and part of his monthly bill was a £20 item for ultrasound treatment.

The owner duly sent a cheque to the trainer, along with a note explaining why the amount was £20 short: "I'll pay for most things," said the note, "but I refuse to pay for the sodding music."

☺   ☺   ☺

Amateur rider Gavin Wragg was called before the stewards after a hunter chase at Folkestone for dropping his hands and being beaten in a close finish.

After fining him, the senior stewards suggested that the owner of the horse must be very cross.

"Yes he is," said Wragg. "In fact, I'm bloody furious."

☺   ☺   ☺

Two betting inspectors were trying to infiltrate an illegal gambling ring run in a bar.

The undercover men attempted to blend in to the background by dressing down and drinking with the locals.

When they had targetted the man they believed to be taking the illegal bets one asked him: "How do you bet on the big race?"

"Ten to one bar two" he was told.

"Which two?" asked the undercover man.

"You and your bloody mate."

☺   ☺   ☺

"I didn't realise I had such a valuable horse until I heard the auctioneer describe him."

......Robert Morley, actor/owner.

☺   ☺   ☺

As leader amateur rider Tom Tate prepared to ride Badsworth Boy in a Triumph Hurdle prep-race at market Rasen he asked the horse's South Yorkshire owners what they thought were the dangers:

"Eh, lad, there's no danger — joost thee falling off!"

☺   ☺   ☺

After seeing the 56 year old maestro, Lester Piggott, ride his horse, Rodrigo De Triano, to victory in the 1992 2,000 Guineas at Newmarket, owner Robert Sangster was quoted as saying, "Lester Piggott must be the greatest jockey of this century. Probably of the last 200 years. In fact, of the decade."

☺   ☺   ☺

The two owners with more money than sense had each bought a horse at the racehorse sales but were now unsure as to how to tell them apart when they took them back to their stables.

"I know — mine's the one with the plaited tail," said one.

"Don't be stupid, they've both got plaited tails," said the other.

"Er, well, mine's the one wearing blinkers."

"They've both got blinkers, you idiot."

"Well then, I'll have the one with the sheepskin noseband on."

"They've both got sheepskin nosebands on, twit."

"Oh, I give up then. You'll just have to have the grey one and I'll have the black one."

THE RACECOURSE

Trackside tomfoolery

The avid racegoer was about to enter Ascot racecourse when a funeral passed by.

The racegoer stopped, removed his hat and placed it over his heart, bowing his head.

Fellow racegoers were very impressed at this touching scene and one of them standing alongside told him so.

"Well, it was the least I could do, she was always a good wife to me. She had one big fault though — she hated horse racing."

The racegoer was strolling out of Sandown Park when he spotted a huddled figure on the pavement, holding out his hand for a donation.

Taking pity on the forlorn tramp the racegoer, who had backed a winner or two, dropped three fivers into the outstretched hand, admonishing him: "Now, don't waste it on booze, buy yourself some food or get a bed for the night."

"Bollocks," snarled the tramp "I'll do what I like with it — I don't bloody tell you not to go racing, do I?"

☺   ☺   ☺

At a Haydock meeting many years ago a long run of losing favourites looked certain to come to an end in a race where a 'good thing', especially laid out for the occasion, was due to oblige.

Digging deep, punters plunged their remaining resources on the animal, which consequently started red hot favourite.

In a close finish it looked like the favourite had just held on, but the name of a 20/1 shot went up in the frame.

Disgruntled backers rushed to argue with the judge. Even the clerk of the course had, albeit strictly against the rules, backed the favourite, and he said to the judge: "That must have been a very close decision, mustn't it?"

"Yes," replied the judge "and that's the first winner I've backed for weeks."

☺   ☺   ☺

Just before the 'off' of the big race the Chief Steward spotted the trainer giving his horse something.

"What was that, trainer?" asked the Steward.

"Oh, just a harmless lump of sugar. Look, I'll eat some myself."

Not convinced, the Steward asked to try a lump of the sugar for himself.

As the jockey prepared to load the horse into the stalls the trainer whispered to him: "Go straight to the front and stay there. It's a certainty, you can't get beat.

"And don't worry if you hear something coming up behind

you — it'll only be me or the Chief Steward."

☺   ☺   ☺

The punter was so ecstatic at having backed a winner that he rushed into the Winner's Enclosure and planted a huge, smacking kiss on the horse which had just brought about such a dramatic increase in his fortunes.

The gesture was not well received by the horse's snooty owner, who looked down his nose at the punter, called for security men to have him ejected and said: "I say, what damnably disgraceful behaviour, you oik. How dare you do that to my horse?"

Replied the elated punter, "Terribly sorry, old boy, I thought it was your wife."

☺   ☺   ☺

The racegoer was walking past a bookie's pitch when he suffered a heart attack, collapsed and died.

A doctor was called, but there was nothing he could do.

"Well, we'd better stop taking bets out of respect," said the bookie.

But a minute later he was shouting the odds as loudly as ever with the prostrate body still laid out in front of him awaiting the arrival of an ambulance.

"I thought you'd stopped taking bets out of respect," said the doctor.

"And so I did," said the bookie. "But Doc, we only allow two minutes silence for all the dead of two World Wars, for God's sake."

☺   ☺   ☺

The keen racegoer finally died. He found himself standing at the pearly gates trying to gain entry past the resident 'Jobsworth', who was wearing a small bowler hat and standing next to a notice reading, 'No jeans allowed'.

"Do you think I might come in?" asked the racegoer.

The gateman explained that Heaven had just introduced a quota system — so many lawyers, so many doctors, so many grocers, so many racing people — and the quota of racegoers had just been fulfiled for the year.

"Mm," said the racegoer "well, what if I could persuade somebody to leave — could I have his place?"

"Persuade somebody to leave Heaven? No one's ever done that before. Mind you, there's no rule against it. I suppose you could have a try. "Remember, though, you're on a twenty four hour pass and if you don't succeed by then you'll have to come out and go to Hell — or Epsom, as we call it."

The racegoer shuddered and went in. He soon found Heaven's Racing Section where he was greeted by ghosts, phantoms and spirits anxious for recent news of the racing scene back on the mortal coil.

"Oh, its much the same, you know, Lester's made another comeback, Pipe's trained five hundred winners, they've changed the rules of the Jockey Championship again...."

Draining the last of his pint of ambrosia, the punter looked thoughtful and said: "I did hear something on the way up, though — they're opening up a thirty day meeting in Hell with guaranteed prize money of £100,000 for each race and guaranteed odds of at least 10/1 the field in each race of eight runners or less — they're even staging a Derby of Derbies with Shergar, Sea Bird, Relko, Troy and Slip Anchor running in it."

Suddenly, there was a great commotion as angels, cherubs, spirits, ghosts and phantoms made a dash for the exit.

Laughing, the racegoer looked around him. "That's me in, then. I suppose most of the others will be back soon and I can spend a pleasurable eternity discussing racing."

But two days passed, then a week, and no-one had returned.

Mystified, the racegoer wandered back to the pearly gates for a chat with the gatemen. "Any of the lads back, yet?" he asked the Jobsworth.

"Not one" he was told. "They shot out of here like Bats out of Hell. It looks like you're safely in for good now."

"Mm," pondered the racegoer. "You know, I reckon there just might have been something in that story I told them after all."

And he dashed past the Jobsworth looking for the road to Hell.

☺   ☺   ☺

Bill and Bert were crossing the racecourse on their way home after a day at the races at which they had lost all their punting money and over-indulged themselves on the booze.

It was becoming dark and the crowds had dispersed. As they began to walk across, Bert grabbed Bill's arm and rushed him to the other side of the track.

"Hey, what are you doing?" demanded Bill.

"We've gotta be careful," slurred Bert. "That bloody horse we backed in the last race — well he's probably still running out here somewhere."

☺   ☺   ☺

"I'm hear to skin these bookies and make a small fortune," announced the racegoer.

"There's only one way you'll ever do that," said a passer-by to him. "And that's by starting with a large one."

☺ ☺ ☺

Walking amongst the assembled ranks of the bookies during the big race meeting a punter suddenly spotted a bundle on the floor.

He quickly bent down and picked it up and was shocked to discover that it was a thick roll of tenners, held together by an elastic band.

Being basically an honest type, the punter shouted out: "Excuse me, has anyone lost a roll of banknotes with a rubber band round them?"

A stampede of racegoers charged towards the punter.

First to arrive was an elderly gent who was asked by the punter: "Describe what you've lost."

"Well, there were about a hundred ten pound notes with a blue elastic band around them."

"Yes," said the punter "that's exactly right, you're very lucky, I've found your elastic band."

☺ ☺ ☺

The two crooked racecourse tipsters met towards the end of the meeting.

One told the other: "I've found a great punter — he's loaded and he's been putting a hundred quid for me on every tip I've given him.

"The only trouble is they've all got beat. He's had five losers in a row. What do you reckon I should do now?"

"Give him up," advised his mate. "He's obviously a jinx."

☺ ☺ ☺

A racehorse walked up to the on-course bookie and asked for a tenner on himself.

The bookie looked amazed.

"What's the matter?" asked the horse "haven't you ever heard of a talking horse?"

"Its not that," said the bookie "I just can't believe you think you can win."

☺   ☺   ☺

A horse called Coffee suddenly attracted some huge bets just before the race was about to start.

It was backed down from 16/1 to 4/1 and having just taken some stiff wagers for it the bookie decided he'd have to lay some of his liabilities off.

"Quick, go and get 4's Coffee," he ordered his clerk, handing him a thick wad of notes.

The clerk decided to take a chance that the horse would be beaten and stuffed the money into his wallet.

Coffee stormed home by ten lengths.

Realising he was now in big trouble, the clerk thought quickly and walked back to the bookie's stand with four cups of tea on a tray.

As the bemused bookmaker stared at him the clerk said:

"Sorry, they'd run out of coffee so I got four teas instead — here's your change."

☺   ☺   ☺

The racecourse bookie found an unopened pay packet accidentally dropped by a racegoer.

He picked up the paypacket, opened it and groaned.

"What's the matter, mate?" asked his clerk "you've had a right result there."

"A result? Are you joking — have you seen the bloody tax those bastards have stopped me?"

☺   ☺   ☺

As one racegoer said to the other en route to the track: "I

hope I break even this afternoon — I could do with the money."

☺   ☺   ☺

The famous TV compere, presenter of 'What's My Line' was enjoying a day at the races when he decided he would place a hefty wager.

He walked up to one of the bookies with his wad of money which he was looking to stick on a 10/1 shot, only to be told that the layer would only take £50 of the bet.

"Do you know who I am?" asked the compere.

"Course I do, mate — you're on that What's My Line programme — great show."

"Well, how would you like to be on it?"

"Yeah, great."

"You'll do well — nobody would ever guess you're supposed to be a bookmaker."

☺   ☺   ☺

It was the racegoer's 66th birthday on June 6, the sixth day of the sixth month in 1966.

Checking the racecard he noticed that in the sixth race, horse number six was named Lucky Six and was quoted at 6/1.

He rushed to the nearest bookie and staked £6 on the horse — it finished sixth!

☺   ☺   ☺

The bookie and his tic-tac man were half-way through the meeting when the tic-tac man suddenly collapsed and died.

"Oh God, how am I going to break the news to his wife?" thought the bookie as he rang her to let her know.

As she answered he just blurted out: "Your husband's

dropped dead with a heart attack."

"No — he hasn't!" she gasped.

"Wanna bet?"

☺   ☺   ☺

There was one race to go. The racegoer had backed a couple of winners and enjoyed more than a few glasses of bubbly in celebration.

He suddenly realised that the runners were coming to the last fence in the last race of the day so he rushed up to the top step of the grandstand to get a better view.

Slightly the worse for wear, he missed his footing and tumbled back down the steps, falling heavily, cutting his head as he went and sending a number of innocent bystanders flying.

Waking up the next morning in hospital, he began to come round slowly, remembering what had happened.

In the bed next to him, with his leg hoisted up in the air and plastered from ankle to thigh, was an elderly gentleman.

"And what happened to you?" asked the racegoer.

"You'll never believe it, but I was at the races yesterday and I was up in the grandstand watching the last race when some bloody drunk fell down the steps and took half the stand with him. What happened to you?"

☺   ☺   ☺

The wealthy racegoer was on his way into Royal Ascot when he was accosted by a scruffy, dirty tramp: "Spare the cash for a cup of tea, guv?"

Touched by the tramp's plight the punter said: "I'll do better than that. Come in to the races with me and have a drink or two."

"Sorry, sir, I don't drink."

"Oh. Never mind, then, have one of my favourite Havana cigars."

"Sorry, sir, I don't smoke."

"Oh dear. Well, listen, I've just been given a 'good thing' for the last race. Put every penny you can beg on it — and here's a tenner to start the ball rolling."

"Sorry, sir, I don't gamble. All I want is a cup of tea."

"And you shall have it — come on, I'm taking you straight to my home right now — I want my wife to see for herself just what happens to a man who doesn't drink, doesn't smoke and doesn't gamble."

☺   ☺   ☺

Watching the horses parading before the race, spectators were astonished to see one of the runners plodding round wearing four brown boots, one on each foot.

One of the bemused racegoers asked the trainer: "Why is your horse wearing brown boots?"

"Because his black ones are at the cobbler's."

☺   ☺   ☺

The fanatical racegoer was on his way home after another losing day at the sports. He didn't even have the fare home, so he thumbed a lift.

A Rolls Royce stopped for him and he jumped into the chauffeur-driven car, whose wealthy occupant listened to the racegoer's tale of woe before delivering him a lecture on the evils of the turf in general and gambling in particular — after which he handed him £50 which he made him promise to hand straight over to his wife for housekeeping.

A couple of weeks later the same chap was returning

from Sandown Park, potless once again and again thumbing a lift, when along came the same Rolls Royce as before.

This time the wealthy moralist was even more irate when the racegoer admitted he had again strayed off the straight and narrow.

"Here's £50, take it straight home to your wife — and don't make the same mistake again."

He might as well have saved his breath. A few days later, on his way past Ascot racecourse, the loaded philanthropist observed the persistent punter yet again holding his thumb out waiting for a lift.

But, as soon as the racegoer spotted the Roller, he broke into a jog and began to run away, shouting: "Keep away from me — you're a bloody jinx — every time you give me a lift I end up losing money."

The unlucky racegoers had backed five consecutive losers.

With just one race remaining one punter said to the other: "That priest over there — he's been making a sign over one horse in each race, then backing it, and he's had five winners."

The punters decided to watch the priest closely and back the horse over which he made the sign this time with all their remaining cash.

Sure enough, he made the sign, they backed the horse and it dashed into a clear lead in the race when suddenly, with only yards to run, it collapsed and died.

Devastated, the punters went over and spoke to the priest, explaining that they had decided to back the horse because he had made a sign over it.

Said the priest: "That's the trouble with you atheists — you can't tell the difference between a blessing and the last rites."

☺   ☺   ☺

What's the definition of a pessimist? An optimist on his way home from the races.

☺   ☺   ☺

Extract from a commentary at Sandown racecourse on Saturday, August 31, 1991: "Hymn Book being held up at the back by Willie Carson."

☺   ☺   ☺

Desperate to get into Royal Ascot, the racegoer grudgingly paid over £200 in tenners to the ticket tout for a £20 ticket.

"That ticket looks like it might be forged to me," said the racegoer's friend.

"That's okay — so were the tenners."

☺   ☺   ☺

It was Derby Day and the once a year bookie on the Epsom Downs realised that he was facing a substantial pay out if the favourite won. Fortunately, he had anticipated just such a problem and brought along with him a few tough 'mates' to protect his interests.

Sure enough, the favourite obliged.

Up came a client with his winning ticket, asking for his £500 winnings.

The bookie called over one of his 'mates' — "Pay him out," said the bookie.

The tough delivered a right hook to the winning punter who was knocked unconscious.

The next winning customer showed a ticket and asked for his due £200.

"Not quite so hard," the bookie told his 'mate' who decked the unfortunate winner.

This continued until the bookie's stand was covered with prone, groaning bodies.

Just one meek looking punter remained, clutching a ticket and trembling.

"Well?" said the bookie "and how much do you want?"

"Who? Me?" stammered the punter "no, I don't want anything at all — I've just brought your ticket back."

☺   ☺   ☺

The racecourse tipster was shouting his own praises: "Last week at this very meeting I tipped EIGHT winners," he bellowed.

"Excuse me," said a passing racegoer "there were only six races last week."

"Didn't you check the results?" demanded the tipster. "There were TWO dead-heats."

☺   ☺   ☺

A *Daily Mail* racing journalist complained that he was refused admission "by an officious security guard" to the Tattersalls enclosure at Newmarket racecourse.

"My crime?" he wrote. "Eating a Twix." And he concluded: "Presumably this is what they call a chocolate bar!"

☺   ☺   ☺

The Stewards Enquiry following the last race had gone on for over an hour and those involved were anxious to depart.

"Everyone's getting damned impatient," said the Senior Steward to his assistant.

"Anyway, I've got an appointment this evening and I want to get away — let's refer the case to the Jockey Club.

"Blast it, we've missed the post now, can't send the paperwork to them."

"Fax it up, my Lord," suggested the assistant helpfully.

"Mm, does rather, doesn't it?" mused the Senior Steward.

BOOKIES
& PUNTERS

Gambling gags & betting banter

The regular losing punter called into the betting shop and asked to see the manager.

"I'm sorry, sir, he died yesterday," said the counter clerk.

The next day the losing punter called in again and again asked to see the manager.

"Sir, I told you yesterday, he's dead," the cashier repeated.

On the third day the punter called in yet again and once more asked to see the manager.

The cashier finally lost her temper: "Look, if I've told you once I've told you three times — he's bloody well dead."

"Yes, I know," said the punter "but I just love to hear you say that."

☺   ☺   ☺

Searching through her husband's pockets for some spare cash, the wife came across a slip of paper with a message scrawled upon it: 'Charlotte 3.15. Wednesday'.

Convinced that her husband must be having an affair she confronted him and demanded to know the meaning of the message.

Thinking fast the husband calmed his wife down and told her that the slip of paper was to remind him of a tip he'd had for a horse.

Breathing a mental sigh of relief he went off to work.

Returning home that evening, looking forward to his dinner he was somewhat miffed to have it hurled at him as he walked through the door.

Wiping the meat and two veg from his face he demanded to know what was the matter.

"Your bloody horse rang up," screamed his wife "to say she was awfully bloody sorry but she couldn't make the 3.15 on Wednesday."

Dave The Punter was Bert The Bookie's best customer — and with good reason. His average stake on a horse was £1,000 and he invariably backed the most broken down old nags who would get beat by miles, but as long as his horse got a mention or two on the SIS commentary he wasn't too worried and would pay up promptly.

One day Dave rang Bert and told him he wanted £5,000 on a 100/1 no-hoper in the last race of the day.

"Couldn't win if it started yesterday," said Dave. "But 'er indoors likes the name — Right Royal."

Bert accepted the bet, which he decided not to bother laying off. However, just to make sure Dave enjoyed losing his money he rang up SIS and spoke to the commentator who was covering the race, asking him to make sure he mentioned Right Royal at some stage of the proceedings no matter how far behind the rest he was.

The race duly started, but there was neither sight nor sound of Right Royal as they came to the final fence.

Bert was happy that he was about to become £5,000 richer but a little miffed that his phone call had failed to produce even a token mention of Right Royal to humour Dave when the commentator suddenly became very excited and began to shout: "As they come to the final fence Right Royal is beginning to make ground hand over fist — as they jump it and land on the run in Right Royal has gone a length clear, two lengths clear, three lengths clear — and I'm not bloody joking, Bert, he's bloody well won by four lengths."

At the 1961 Derby the vast majority of bookies had a great afternoon as the big race winner Psidium was an almost unbackable 66/1 shot. However, one bookie was faced with a punter who had staked a tenner on the outsider and explained delightedly to the underwhelmed layer that he used to serve on a ship called Psidium.

Replied the bookie: "What a pity it wasn't the bloody Titanic."

At a jumps meeting in the West Country before the First World War two army officers invested their all with a bookie on the final race of the day. As their fancy came bounding to the last fence a distance clear, so they noticed the bookie rapidly disappearing in the opposite direction.

Giving chase they collared him outside the course and 'persuaded' him none too gently to hand over their winnings.

Returning to the course they discovered that their horse had tumbled over at the last and been beaten.

☺   ☺   ☺

Bookmaker Herbert King, who died in 1993, had written his own epitaph, which was published in the *Sporting Life*:

Here lies the body of old bookie Bert
Who deprived many a punter of his Sunday shirt
But at last he lies beneath the dirt
The one tip in life he said was a 'cert'.

☺   ☺   ☺

Honest Joe the Bookie had a customer who regularly backed long priced winners and made a good living out of the game.

When Honest Joe died suddenly his partner, Long Odds Fred, took over the business and with it the account of the lucky punter, Jim.

Shortly after, Jim the punter fell ill and was rushed into hospital where it was discovered that he required urgent surgery.

Just before he was to carry out the life or death operation, the surgeon came in to see Jim to ask him if he was prepared for the ordeal.

"I am," said Jim "but could you do me a favour? — ring up my bookie and tell him I want a grand on Foinavon in the National — it'll be a 100/1 shot."

The surgeon duly went off to ring Long Odds Fred.

"This is the surgeon at the hospital. Jim the lucky punter is my patient. I am about to operate on him and I'm not so sure he'll be able to pull through. "He's asked me to put £1,000 on Foinavon for him in this afternoon's Grand

National."

"Oh, has he?" said Long Odds Fred "then you tell him from me to wait a couple of hours and put his bloody bet on with Honest Joe."

☺   ☺   ☺

The man walked into the betting shop clutching four small pebbles and demanding to put them all on Red Rum to win the Grand National.

The manager laughed and explained to the man that they did not accept stones and that he would need cash to place a bet.

But the man insisted on staking his pebbles, so, to humour him, the manager took the pebbles and gave him a betting slip in return.

Sure enough, Red Rum won the National and the pebble punter duly turned up for his winnings. Thinking fast, the manager told his counter clerk to go out into the shop's back yard and fill a bag with gravel which he solemnly handed over to the delighted punter.

A few days later the punter was back — struggling under the weight of a large boulder which he lifted on to the counter.

The manager looked up at him and then at the boulder and said: "Oh, no, I'm not taking that, I'm not stupid, you must have had a tip for one."

☺   ☺   ☺

A man with a stammer walked into the betting shop and said to the manager: "I've b-b-b-backed a f-f-f—five t-t-t......"

"Five to two?" asked the bookie, trying to be helpful.

"N-n-n-no," said the man "I've b-b-b-backed a f-f-five t-t-t......"

"Five to one?" said the bookie, becoming a little impatient."

"N-n-n-no," said the man "I've b-b-b-backed......"

"Oh, bloody hell, mate, give it a rest," said the bookie. "Look, I'm too busy at the moment, take this score and shove off, I'll settle up properly with you later."

"Okay, th-th-th-thanks," stuttered the man and walked out of the shop.

On the way out he was joined by another departing punter, who asked him: "Well, what DID you back then?"

"I b-b-bloody well b-b-bbacked a f-f-ffive t-t—ton lorry into his c-c-c-car."

☺   ☺   ☺

"My bookie and I have a Siamese twin relationship — we're joined at the wallet."

☺   ☺   ☺

The two gamblers met up — one looking very smart in a brand new suit.

"I got it by backing a horse," he told his friend.

"Oh, where?"

"Through Burton's window."

☺   ☺   ☺

The old lady walked up to the racecourse bookie to place her small bet.

"Do you want it each way, dear?" asked the layer.

"Each way? Do I have to back it going to the start as well as coming back?"

☺   ☺   ☺

The competitive bookie would never be outdone. If the

bookie next to him chalked up 2/1, he would quote 9/4. If the opposition went 3/1, he had to be 7/2.

Then the bookie took up golf. Seeing him out on the course one day an acquaintance asked his partner how the bookie was getting on.

"Not bad," he said. "But there's just one snag — we can't get him to shout 'Fore' — he keeps yelling 'Nine to two'."

☺   ☺   ☺

The punter had been given a very hot tip for a horse by a trainer.

"Back my horse, Lunch, it won't be beaten."

Next day the punter decided to go and back the horse and he called in for a swift half on the way to the betting shop. Eight pints later he was well away when all of a sudden he remembered he hadn't placed his bet, and he couldn't remember the name of the horse, either.

Looking up from his beer he saw a sign saying, 'Lunch 12-1'.

That was it — and what a good price, too. He said to the barman: "Can you get me a tenner on that horse there, Lunch, at 12-1, mate?"

The barman, assuming he'd had one too many, slung him out.

Staggering into the pub next door the punter saw another sign — this one bearing the legend 'Lunch, 11-2'.

"Oh, no, they're backing it and I've missed the price," he said, frantically calling the barman over and demanding that he be laid the 12-1.

Once again he was chucked out.

Into the next pub he tottered, only to see 'Lunch, 1-2'.

"Oh shit, I'm buggered if I'll back it now — its gone odds on," he muttered.

Just then a waitress emerged, holding a plate and calling: "Sausages, one."

The punter sighed in relief and said: "Great, Lunch got beat. Thank God I didn't get on."

☺   ☺   ☺

The two Jewish punters met on the way home from the races.

Hymie had backed four long-odds winners. Abie, by contrast, had managed to find only losers.

"So, tell me, how do you do it?" said Abie to Hymie.

"It's very simple. Before I go to the track I go and pray in the synagogue and I never fail to back at least four winners a day."

Abie, whose adherence to his religion had lapsed some-what over the years, decided he had little to lose and set off for the nearest synagogue.

He spent an hour a day praying in the synagogue for the next week then, in confident mood, he set off for the race track.

Every single bet he made was a loser.

On the way home he once again met up with Hymie, who was looking very pleased with himself.

"I backed four more winners," beamed Hymie. "How did you get on?"

"No good, all I backed was losers again," moaned Abie.

"But didn't you take my advice and pray at the syna-gogue?" asked Hymie.

"Yes, I did — but, nothing," said Abie.

Hymie thought for a while. "I can't understand this," he said. "Tell me, which synagogue did you say your prayers in?"

"Well," said Abie "the one in Golders Green, of course."

"Oy veh," said Hymie. "Golders Green. What kind of a schmo are you? My life, doesn't everyone know that Golders Green is only for greyhound racing?"

☺   ☺   ☺

A born loser, the gambler finally realised his luck was not about to change, and packed in betting.

Some months later a pal told him he had an absolute certainty. Against his better judgement the born loser decided to give it one more try, so he drew out a hundred quid from his bank account and went off to the betting shop to back the tip.

He waited for the commentary of the race in which his horse, Blackie, a 20/1 shot, was running.

It was a steeplechase and as the race progressed the commentator suddenly said:

"There's a fog coming down here and with two to jump the favourite is in front, but Blackie is gaining on him and challenging strongly.... now they've gone into the mist and I can't pick them out.... now they're coming out of the fog and approaching the last — it's the favourite and Blackie together.... and as they come to the last they've disappeared back into thick fog and, yes, one of them has fallen, but I can't tell which one...."

At this point the born loser jumped to his feet and bellowed: "That bloody commentator — he's only a couple of hundred yards away from the race and he can't make out which horse falls — me, I'm a couple of hundred MILES away, and I bloody well KNOW which bloody horse has fallen."

☺   ☺   ☺

The punter's creed: "You don't gamble to win — you

gamble so you can gamble the next day."

☺ ☺ ☺

Then there was the compulsive gambler who was chucked out Gamblers Anonymous for trying to bet on how long it would take him to give it up.

☺ ☺ ☺

Studying his racecard the punter asked a bookie: "What will I get if Rubber wins at 10/1, Elastic at 11/1 and Springy at 12/1?"
"A cheque that bounces."

☺ ☺ ☺

The champion jockey's mount in the big race was beaten by a short head.
As he dismounted from the horse, the champion was punched on the nose by an angry punter who had lost money by backing him.
In court later, the punter said that his twin brother, who had also backed the horse, had volunteered to carry out the attack on the jockey, but that he always preferred to stick it on the nose rather than rely on cross doubles.

☺ ☺ ☺

Two punters were discussing the outcome of the last race:
"That horse I backed must be bloody good."
"How's that, then? It was well beat."
"Ah yes — but it took twenty other horses to do it."

☺ ☺ ☺

The bookie asked the old lady how she regularly backed a winner a day.
"I stick a pin in the *Sporting Life*," she said.

Next day she backed a winning treble and again the bookie asked her how she'd done it.

"I couldn't find the pin so I used a fork."

☺   ☺   ☺

Joe had frequented the same betting shop for a quarter of a century, yet he'd never yet managed to show a profit on a day's racing bets.

When the betting shop's head office heard about this they decided to name Joe the country's unluckiest punter and to hold a small ceremony at which they would present him with a free bet to make up for his disappointments over the years.

Having called a press conference, the shop company's public relations man announced that he was going to tear a betting slip into ten pieces and write a different amount on each, from £10 to £1,000.

These would be put into the company managing director's bowler hat and Joe would draw one out, winning the relevant free bet.

As the cameras flashed Joe put his hand into the hat and drew out his free bet.

"Well, which one have you drawn?" asked the PR man.

Replied Joe: "6 7/8"

☺   ☺   ☺

The racegoer on holiday in Italy is passing the Vatican.

He decides to pop in to see the Pope but is told by an aide that His Holiness is unavailable.

He tries on three consecutive days, getting the same answer.

On the final attempt the aide tells the man: "Sadly, the Pope has passed on — that's, of course, why you can't see him, but we did not wish to release this news to the world just yet, so we would appreciate it if you would say nothing."

The man returns home and rushes straight to the local bookmaker and takes odds of 100/1 about the Pope dying before the end of the week.

On his way out of the betting shop the punter sees an old man sobbing his heart out.

"What's the matter?" he asks.

The old man tells him he has lost everything and cannot afford to pay his bills.

"Listen, don't tell anyone else, but I've got a certainty for you. I'll lend you a tenner — put it on the Pope being announced dead by the end of the week."

Sure enough, the announcement of the Pope's demise is made, and the man goes to the betting shop to collect his winnings.

On the way out he meets the old man again, but he is still sobbing his heart out.

"What's the matter? You must have won a fortune. Didn't you put the bet on?"

"Yes, I did," said the old man. "But I doubled up the Pope with Lester Piggott."

☺   ☺   ☺

If gambling is so great how come you never see horses betting on people?

☺   ☺   ☺

The punter rang his bookie to discover the result of the 2.30 on a very wet day.

"It was abandoned, sir," said the telephonist.

"Oh really, and what price did that return?"

☺   ☺   ☺

He was one of the unluckiest punters the bookie had ever known and one day the pair of them caught the same train home from the track.

"How's it been going?" asked the bookie.

"Don't ask" said the punter, "I'm down to my last two quid, I've had a disastrous afternoon."

The bookie had had a good afternoon and was in a sympathetic mood, so decided to help out his friend the punter.

"Listen," said the bookie "tell you what I'll do for you — there's evening racing tonight, I'll give you a chance to get a few bob back.

"I'll lay you well over the odds whichever one you fancy in the first. Look, the top weight is the 3/1 favourite in the paper — you can have 6/1 about that one to your two quid — and this one here, he's won his last three races — they make it a 5/1 shot — to you, 10/1 — or this one here, a dual course and distance winner, its 8/1 — you can have 16/1."

"What price will you lay me the bottom weight?"

"That thing — it hasn't been placed for four years, it could-n't win if it started now, you can have 1,000/1."

"Right, that'll do me — I'll have my two quid on that one."

The race was on the radio and, sure enough, the punter's no-hoper stormed home and the bookie, not feeling quite so sympathetic any longer, duly paid over two grand.

The punter arrived home and his wife, thinking she already knew the answer, asked him how he'd done.

"Lousy, as usual. Didn't have a winner all day until the first evening race, then I managed to find the winner all right but, would you believe it, all I had on the bloody thing was a lousy two quid!"

☺   ☺   ☺

The bookie had had a good week and decided to go to church to give thanks.

While he was there the collection plate came round and he duly shoved on a great handful of notes.

As he left the church following the service the Vicar came over to him and said: "You are extremely generous but we couldn't possibly accept that much from one person."

"Listen, take what you can and lay the rest off," said the bookie.

☺   ☺   ☺

A win double seems to be the most perfect bet of them all. It was obviously invented by a punter who felt that one winner wasn't enough, and keenly encouraged by bookies who believe that one loser isn't enough.

☺   ☺   ☺

The novice punter was discussing what happens to horses when they finish their racing careers. He pointed out the horse he was about to back and said, "He'll no doubt enjoy a life of luxury at stud eventually."

"Hardly likely," said his friend, "That horse is a gelding."

"So what's wrong with breeding geldings — they seem to win their fair share of races."

☺   ☺   ☺

A racecourse bookie was taken ill and rushed to hospital. After racing, several fellow bookies went to visit him to enquire after his health, taking with them small presents. The next day when they visited him they saw a large notice over his pillow: "Minimum 5 pounds taken."

☺   ☺   ☺

Asked once why he made so many inauspicious films, actor Peter O"Toole replied, "It's my profession. It's what I do for a living. Anyway, I've got bookies to keep."

☺   ☺   ☺

Overheard in the betting ring at the racecourse following a betting dispute: "We can't talk our way out of this one, we'll have to pay."

☺   ☺   ☺

The big punter had a really hot tip for a horse which he decided to pass on to his best friend who seldom bet. They decided to put 1,000 pounds each on the horse and went to the track to watch the race.

The big punter's friend was something of a novice race-goer and the big punter had to explain to him what was happening.

All was going well and the tip was just coming to win his race when the jockey, going flat out to ride a big finish, dropped his whip and was beaten by a short head.

"I am sorry," the big punter said. "The jockey lost his whip and was beaten."

"Lost his whip!" shouted his friend. "Lost his fucking whip! He can buy a new one for a quid — what about me? I've lost a fucking grand!"

☺   ☺   ☺

Discussing the latest doping sensation, which had seen a hot favourite finish stone last, one punter said to the other: "Why would anyone in their right mind need to risk doping a favourite or go to the expense of bribing the jockey when they could just ask me to back it for them to stop it?"

☺   ☺   ☺

The mother and her young daughter were out shopping in the High Street when, suddenly, a riderless racehorse went careering down the road, hotly pursued by a group of people chasing it.

"Mummy, Mummy, how will they slow that horse down?"

"Quite simple, darling, they'll ask daddy to put ten pounds on it."

☺   ☺   ☺

"Mother," said the knowing little lad "father must have had a bad day at the races yesterday."

"Why do you think that?" asked the fond mother in surprise.

"Well," said the boy with simple logic "my money box won't rattle this morning."

OTHER LANDS

Racing wit from across the water

An Irish trainer was overheard to remark that the only time the Curragh trainers ever get together is for one another's funerals — and then it's to get the horses off the widow.

The Irish priest was stopping passers-by to ask for directions to the church in the unfamiliar town.

"Well, you turn right at the Red Lion, left at the White Horse, left again at the Railway Hotel, then you can't miss it."

The priest looked bemused. He obviously had no idea that these were pub names, so he tried another passer-by.

"No problem, father. Straight down the road as far as Safeway, left there down to Tescos, turn right and go straight down as far as Sainsburys and you can't miss it."

Blank incomprehension once again showed on the face of the Priest who tried a third passer-by.

"Well now, let me think, er, yes, straight down the road as far as Corals, turn left there, straight on as far as the Mecca, then turn left, keep going until you reach William

Hill and its bang opposite, you can't miss it."

"Oh Jesus, t'ank the Lord y'came along m'son. Oid'never have found it otherwise."

☺   ☺   ☺

The Irish trainer was celebrating his horse's victory in a £500 handicap when his pal congratulated him, commenting: "The way he won that race you ought to enter him for the Grand National."

"Now what do you take me for?" asked the trainer.

"If he went and won the Grand National, what sort of weight d'you reckon he'd get in this race next season?"

☺   ☺   ☺

With form lines reading PRUF it was little surprise that the horse started at no-hoper odds of 100/1, but as it jumped the last and drew away to a shock victory an Irish punter was observed shouting and cheering.

"T'be sure, and Oi had all me wages on the nag."

"How come?" asked a baffled punter.

"Well, an' didn't yer horse have the form t'win the race — Promising; Ran well; Unlucky loser; Fit and fancied."

☺   ☺   ☺

Paddy, not the brightest of punters, was celebrating after backing a 100/1 winner.

One of his mates asked him how he'd picked the horse out.

"T'was obvious — the first thing I spotted when I arrived at the racecourse was a number seven on a bookies stand — then I spotted a big advertising banner for Seven Up, then I noticed the seven furlong start."

"But your horse wasn't number seven," said his mate.

"Ah, that's where I was really clever — I'd seen three

sevens, and I said to myself, three sevens are twenty two, so I backed 22 and it bolted in at 7/1."

☺   ☺   ☺

Punters were astonished at the announcement by stewards who quizzed Irish trainer Paddy Mullins following the 20/1 big race win of a horse of his which had recently been beaten at odds on in a two horse race.

The stewards announced that they had accepted Mullins's explanation that he had no explanation.

☺   ☺   ☺

The Irish jockey and his racehorse had been celebrating their big win with a drink or two in a local bar.

The jockey could take his drink but the horse was new to champagne and after his sixth glass was so stoned that he slipped off his stool on to the floor, out for the count.

A few more drinks later, the jockey got up to leave but the barman called over to him: "Oi, what's dat loyin' on d'floor?"

Unsteadily, the jockey walked over to the barman and said: "That's no lion, sir, to be sure, 'tis a racehorse."

☺   ☺   ☺

For some years the Irish trainers Jim Bolger and Dermot Weld fought out a close battle for superiority in terms of the number of winners trained each season, by Weld from his Rosewell House HQ and Bolger from his Colculen base.

The story is told of when the time finally arrives that Weld departs this world and arrives at the pearly gates to be met by St Peter who beckons him in.

A hesitant Weld first ascertains that Bolger has not preceded him and is assured that he hasn't, so deigns to enter.

Taking a stroll around Heaven, Weld is stagered to come across a magnificent palace, painted in purple and white, which he recognises as Bolger's racing colours, and with the name Coolcullen inscribed in large leters above the impressive gates.

Weld quickly returns to St Peter — "I thought you said Bolger wasn't here."

"Nor is he" replies St Peter.

"But I saw a magnificent palace named Coolcullen and painted in his racing colours."

"Aah" said St Peter "No, that's where God lives — you see, he thinks he IS Jim Bolger."

Police hunting for the missing Derby winner Shergar were continuously phoned by an anonymous caller who insisted that they should search the surrounding area around the stud from which he had been spirited away within a two mile radius. Despite being assured that they had done that, the caller continued to ring. Finally the officer in charge of the search spoke to him and asked him why he was so sure that Shergar could be no further than two miles away.

"Sure, an' de horse could never get more that a moile an' six furlongs," was the reply.

Top sports writer Frank Keating tells in his book, *Half Time Whistle*, how: "One Gold Cup morning a few years back I was waiting in St Gregorys for an Irish journo pal who needed to go to confession after Mass. A state of grace is important for winner-picking. He was kneeling, waiting his turn, with a few other like minded and suddenly mea-maximaculpa men. The amiable Benedictine parish priest, of Irish background himself, was getting quickly through the queue of penitents. In goes a ferrety, furtive little stable-lad type.

"'Bless me, Father, for I have sinned,' he begins in a quite audible mutter. Suddenly, from the priest's side of the confessional, a low wail comes, then an exasperated snort — then ripping sounds and a confetti of torn betting slips is tossed through the curtain in fury. It had been plain to hear what words had preceded this storm: 'Forgive me, Father, I've nobbled the favourite for the big one this afternoon.'"

Racing is an international sport and its humour transcends national boundaries, so it is only to be expected that there is a rich seam of laughter to be mined throughout the turf world, and particularly in the United States — as you are about to discover......

"It's easy to grin
When your ship comes in
And life's joys never seem to diminish.
But the lad worth while
Is the guy who can smile
When he's just lost a close photo finish."
Thus wrote Irving Huxley who died aged 89 in 1956.

The racehorse walked into the New York bar and ordered himself a drink.

The bar tender looked up and said, "Hey, buddy, why the

long face?"

After the horse had finished his drink and gone home in came a one-legged jockey.

The barman looked up again: "Hey, Mac, and how are you getting on?"

☺   ☺   ☺

Howard A Rowe, editor of *American Turf Monthly*, told this yarn:

"Some horse players do die broke, and presumably live the same way.

"One such was a steady patron of a Brooklyn pawn shop. One day he appeared with an overcoat to hock.

"The pawnbroker gave him five dollars.

"The next afternoon he was back with a suit of clothes and the proprietor gave him ten dollars.

"The third day he pawned a pair of binoculars, and the fourth day — believe it or not — a pair of shoes.

"That was when the pawnbroker spotted the Racing Form sticking from his hip pocket.

"'What's good today?' he asked."

☺   ☺   ☺

Two well read gentlemen were at Belmont Park race track where, between races, they were discussing the relative merits of various philosophers whilst all around them the horse players were debating the abilities of horses and jockeys. As the two continued to argue heatedly over the likes of Plato, Socrates, Freud and so on, an eavesdropping racegoer glanced up from his racecard and commented: "Hey, you guys certainly believe in putting Descartes before the horse, doncha?"

☺   ☺   ☺

The unsuccessful gambler, distraught at backing yet another loser, had thrown himself from the top level of the grandstand at the New York track.

As he plummeted to the ground with a thump and lay there, a crowd of curious onlookers gathered to gawp.

One spectator, after a few seconds of morbid staring, strolled off, remarking: "There's what I call a sore loser."

☺   ☺   ☺

American owner Jimmy Buchanan was running his mare Head Sea in a final attempt to win a race with the less than successful horse.

His last minute instructions to his jockey were: "If she ain't in the money, keep her."

☺   ☺   ☺

The racegoer was known as the Hard Luck Guy. Everything he touched went to rack and ruin. He NEVER backed a winner — if he did it would be disqualified.

He had spent his entire existence without a shirt on his back. He was a perennial loser.

But one day he told a friend: "I had a good day at the track."

"YOU had a good day?" queried the incredulous pal. "Didja win the double? Didja make a coupla grand?"

The racegoer shook his head. "Nah."

"Didja make a parlay? Maybe ya won a disqualification? What?"

"Well, y'know Old Bill who lives next door to me? He was out at the track, too, today — and he gave me a lift all the way home."

☺   ☺   ☺

The inveterate horse player who never missed a trick with

his bets, was on his death bed.

Friends, who had never realised he was religious, were surprised when he called a rabbi, a minister and a priest to his bedside.

His best friend asked why he had done such a thing and leaned close to the expiring racegoer to hear the answer.

"Hey, ya know me — I'm always looking to hedge my bets," he declared before passing away.

☺   ☺   ☺

He was every trainer's dream owner, paid his bills regular as clockwork even though his horse never came anywhere near winning a race.

When the horse only beat two others home he was quite happy — when it finished in front of four others, almost ecstatic.

The trainer was mystified at this behaviour to the point where he was even becoming suspicious — surely there had to be a reason to explain the owner's unheard of attitude and the reason why each successive dismal failure produced only a nod of the head from the owner as he busily recorded the details in a little note book he always carried around with him.

"What are you writing in that book?" the trainer asked. "And how come you're always so happy when your horse finishes out of the money — this nag has not won enough cash to pay for his daily oats."

"Well," explained the owner, "every time he runs he beats one or two horses, sometimes even more. I am noting down the name of every horse that finishes behind him because one day soon a race is sure to come along with nothing in it except the horses we have beaten.

"And then," he continued exultantly "and then WE BET."

The suit the racegoer was wearing had, to be honest, seen better days — a scarecrow would have thought twice before donning it.

The shirt which went with it and his shoes weren't exactly the height of fashion, either, but he was at the betting window placing a huge wad of cash on an outsider which duly romped home at 20/1.

Congratulating him, an acquaintance pointed out tactfully that perhaps a small percentage of his large winnings might be invested in a new outfit.

"I suppose I do need 'em," he admitted "but, hey, I just don't have the money."

"Whaddya mean you don't have the money — you just collected over three grand, man."

"Why, I couldn't spend that" gasped the outraged horse player, "That's my betting money."

The final day of the New York racing season was approaching and Steve the Stiff had gone seven long months without cashing a bet.

A trainer friend had told him to get all the scratch he could muster and come out on closing day for a sure thing that would pay a big price in the last race on the card.

"It's not my horse," the trainer said "and I can't tell you the name of the horse until they're almost at the post because I'm sworn to secrecy.

"But you be there with a wad of dough, and I'll get you out for the season."

The final day of the season rolled around and by the ninth race Steve was holding five hundred hard dollars he had scraped up from the last available source.

Two minutes to post time the trainer dashed up to him and whispered: "Bet it all on number seven. He's 12/1, and bet to win only."

Steve rushed to the fifty dollar window with only fifteen seconds remaining before the running of the last race that year at Aqueduct.

"Number seven," gasped Steve "ten times."

The seller merely nodded, but made no attempt to punch out the tickets. Steve was fit to be tied and his face showed it.

"What's with you?" he roared. "Where's them tickets?"

The calm, grey-haired gent behind the machine was affable. "I'm Allen Funt," he beamed "and, smile sir, you're on Candid Camera."

The racetracker went to the city bank in an effort to secure a loan to buy himself a racehorse.

"I don't think we could justify lending you $100,000 to buy a racehorse," said the bank official. "But let me have a statement and we'll see what we can do."

"Here's your statement," said the racegoer "I want to own a Kentucky Derby winner."

The keen punter woke up one morning having spent the whole night dreaming of hats.

Deciding it must have been an omen, he rang his bookie and asked him what was running that day with names associated with headgear.

The first six races of the day produced Fedora, Brown Trilby, Top Hat, Sombrero, Stetson Lad and Homburg, but there didn't seem to be any appropriate choice for the final race, according to the bookie, who advised: "I can only suggest you back Cloakroom. That seems to be the nearest and it is sure to start favourite."

The punter duly placed an accumulator bet and went off to work.

Later he rang the bookie to find out how his selections had got on.

"Well, your hat horses have turned out to be real hot horses — the first six have all won and you now have $10,000 running on to Cloakroom in the last — and the result is just coming through, hold on...... oh, gee, Cloakroom is only second, what bad luck."

"Oh well," said the punter "that's the way it goes — tell me, what did win the last?"

"Some French-trained outsider called Chapeau," said the bookie.

On his way home from the track after an unsuccessful afternoon's betting the racegoer heard a voice in his head urging him: "Go to the trotters tonight, Go to the trotters tonight."

He'd never experienced anything like it before and immediately set off towards the nearest trotting track.

Once there the voice in his head advised him to: "Bet number seven, bet number seven."

He did it and it stormed in, paying $20.

The voice urged him to play up his winnings on number three in the next, which he did, winning again.

By the time the last race came around he was $50,000 to the good and the voice was insisting that he: "Bet number two — the whole roll on number two."

Number two's odds crashed down from 10/1 to odds-on

but, as the race progressed, number two gradually fell farther and farther behind, eventually ending up stone last.

The voice in his head returned: "Hey, how about THAT, how about THAT."

The old-timer was holding court to an incredulous audience of youngsters and was recalling the time he had watched a race featuring the then champion mare who was taking part in the race despite being in foal.

"Man, that was some horse — I tell you she was so fast that by the time they reached the back-stretch she was forty, fifty lengths in front — so she stopped and had her foal there and then — and STILL went on to win the race." The audience made disbelieving noises at this point but the old-timer held up his hand and called for silence before declaring: "And believe it or not, the foal finished second."

The old-time jockey was reaching the end of the road, coming to the final stretch. He decided it was time to make a will.

After making arrangements for friends and relatives, he was asked by his lawyer how his body was to be disposed of when he passed on.

"Hey, I tell ya, I want that cremation thing — and when its done I want that you should see that 20 per cent of the ashes are blown in the face of Hymie Schwartz — he's my agent."

☺   ☺   ☺

"I came by the racetrack today but it was closed," actor W

C Fields once told a friend "so I just shoved all my money through the gate."

☺   ☺   ☺

W C Fields was at the racetrack with a friend who pointed out a famous horse to him with the comment: "That horse is worth over a quarter of a million." To which the comedian replied: "How can a dumb animal save up that much dough?"

☺   ☺   ☺

A coup was organised for an obscure Australian course called Canterbury. The horse was All Sorts, ridden by jockey Kelso junior for his father, Kelso senior, who thought the horse was a good thing but was a little concerned as to how he would get his cash on without being rumbled.

En route to the track, Kelso senior stopped off at a hotel where a fellow trainer, Tom Payten, introduced him to a Sydney produce merchant named Patrick Hooligan, who confessed he had never been on a racecourse in his life.

"Then you are the man I've been looking for" said Mr Kelso, who asked Mr Hooligan whether he was willing to help him place his wagers.

Mr Hooligan readily agreed and Mr Kelso handed him £100 with instructions to put the money on All Sorts.

Unfortunately, though, All Sorts was just touched off by Sir Daniel Cooper's Pastmaster — so Mr Kelso was amazed when Mr Hooligan handed him £210, saying: "I did what you told me — I backed All Sorts."

In fact, the novice punter had literally backed all sorts — placing a £10 bet on each of the ten runners and collecting on the 20/1 winner.

The American Jewish father was so desperate to stop his young son gambling that he packed him off to strict boarding school.

A couple of weeks later he sent him a telegram reading: "Don't forget, son, Yom Kippur starts tomorrow."

Back came the son's reply: "Thanks for the tip, Dad, put ten dollars on for me."

☺   ☺   ☺

Greg Wood of *The Independent* told readers in December 1994 that an American track commentator had given him an insight into the way in which US jocks kept their weight down.

"They'll eat a cheeseburger with great gusto, then disappear into the toilets and stick their fingers down their throat.

"They say that if you do it within five minutes, it tastes as nice coming back as it did going down."

☺   ☺   ☺

1930's American trainer 'Whistling' Bob Smith was a real gambler.

In 1942 he suffered a heart seizure and was being taken to hospital by ambulance accompanied by a friend who asked Bob's doctor about his chances of pulling through.

"Only one in ten," said the doctor.

The old trainer, who they had believed to be unconscious, opened his eyes and said he'd take 100 dollars to ten.

Sadly, shortly after, he died.

☺   ☺   ☺

Aussie jockey Athol George Mulley told the story of two North Queensland "battlers" who took a useful horse they owned to run in a provincial race, the Bandiwollop Cup. They thought he was a certainty but by the time they arrived in Bandiwollop they had run out of cash to back him, so borrowed $100 from a local storekeeper who told them he was also the judge at the local racetrack.

A day before the big race the pair heard of the arrival of another ringer which they knew could beat their horse, so they switched their bets on to the newcomer and told their own jockey to settle for second place.

They were pleased to get 6/1 for their money and settled back to watch the race, which went right to plan with their horse just finishing second behind the recent arrival.

However, they were nonplussed to see the number of their horse hoisted into the frame as the winner.

They rushed over to the judge and said, "But our horse was beaten by half a length. What's the idea?"

"Yeah, but how the bloody hell would you pay back my $100 if your horse got beat?"

☺   ☺   ☺

In the 1970s husband and wife jockeys Johnny and Mary Bacon rode against each other in US races. On one occasion the two had a dispute during a race which resulted in Mary receiving a five day suspension: "Okay, I've got five days" commented Mary, "But he's getting five nights!"

☺   ☺   ☺

Australian bookmaker, Bill Waterhouse, once said, "I gamble on the punter rather than the horse. I don't care how good a horse's reputation, if I think the backer is a born loser, I will stand his bet for a fortune."

☺   ☺   ☺

Then there was the American jockey who was booked to

ride for a season for a large French stable. Arriving at the stable, it was realised that he didn't speak a word of French, so a stable lad who spoke both English and French was called in to give the jockey some assistance. The first thing he told the jockey was, "Now the first thing you need to learn is a phrase you'll probably hear from the boss when he gives you a leg up at Longchamp tomorrow — it's 'pas aujourd hui' and it means 'not today'."

PAST TENSE

Racing yarns of yore

In 1938 a book was published which claimed to be full of 'The bubble of laughter and the sparkle of wit.'

It was called, *Punter's Pie*, — 'A book of racing stories collected by William Fawcett'.

Just as fashion dates very quickly, it is interesting to read through this book and to realise how humour, too, can change over the years.

Here I have chosen a few of the stories from the volume to illustrate what was considered likely to encourage 'rollicking laughter' the best part of sixty years ago.......

One of the best jokes in the book appeared in Mr Fawcett's introduction, in which he commented that during the compilation of the tome: "I've had me Epsom Downs".

The first yarn in the book got it off to a promising start: "This one belongs to Manchester. A horse ran at one of the jumping meetings there, and was palpably not trying very hard to win.

"He wore heavy cottonwool bandages and as he returned to scale the jockey kept glancing down anxiously at the horse's forelegs.

"'Don't look at his legs', bawled a disappointed backer, ''ave a look at 'is mouth an' see if 'is poor bloomin' jaw's broken'."

☺   ☺   ☺

We move on to a story about an owner who wrote to his trainer: "My horse has been under your care for three months. Do you think he can stay?" Came the reply: "Dear Sir, Your horse can stay all right, but he takes a damned long time about it."

☺   ☺   ☺

On Page 17, though, comes the first hint that the humour of a bygone age may not quite translate to the present day:

"In the (eighteen) nineties one of the racing celebrities was Fred Swindells, or 'Lord Freddy' as he was more usually called.

"He started life as boots in a Lancashire hotel and rose to a position of great wealth on the Turf.

One day he was interviewed by a 'reporter' as 'Lord Freddy' called him, for he never forgot his Northern birth.

"'To what,' asked the 'reporter', 'to what qualities do you attribute your rise to wealth, Mr Swindells?'

"'To thrift, sobriety and hard work,' replied 'Lord Freddy'.

"'Don't you include honesty as well?' asked the seeker after news.

"'Well, yes,' said 'Lord Freddy', rather dubiously, 'perhaps a little honesty as well.'"

☺   ☺   ☺

Can you feel those ribs being tickled? No? Well try this one:

"One of the most gallant riders and best of sportsmen was

the late Count Charles Kinsky who won the Grand National on his own mare Zoedone. The year before Lord Manners had triumphed on Seaman and, as the Count and Zoedone went back to scale, one steeplechase jockey said to another, "'Larst year a Lord wins it, now a bloomin' foreign Count gets 'ome — who the 'ell next I wonder? Maybe an old woman in petticuts.'

"'Quite true,' said the Count with a smile, 'and I hope, Jimmy, the the old woman will be yourself.'"

Of course, these days there is no such thing as a division of the classes on the turf, is there? And now:

"Two stable lads met in a public house. They were employed by rival stables, both of which were to be represented in a big race in the near future.

"One of the lads bragged very loudly of the chance of his stable's candidate, but the other merely reiterated that the horse from his stable had already beaten the other, giving weight away.

"When he had recovered from his stupefaction at this statement, the bragger pointed out that there might be other very good horses in the race.

"'Well,' said the other lad quietly 'in that case our horse'll have to break into a gallop.'"

Amusing, that one, certainly — but this next, I found incomprehensible:

"I was witness to this one. At Epsom a few years back a huge crowd was standing round a bookie who, with lungs of brass, was shouting 'Nine to four the feald, nine to four the feald.'

"One of the never-say-die brigade, standing in the middle of the motley throng, shouted, ''Ere,' Arry, I'll take yer'

"The bookie replied, 'Shove yer dough up then and it's a bet.'

"'I can't get me 'ands up,' was the reply."

I turned the page over to find the punchline — but that was it!

☺   ☺   ☺

The next story shows that some things don't change — it is basically the 'spiel' of a racecourse tipster from those days:

"An' if I'm not telling you people the truth, the 'ole truth, and nothin' but the truth, I'll give a cheque for a fasand pahnds to the H'Epsom Cottage 'Orsepittle.

"Only this very morning, King George the Fifth 'e sends for me.

"'Charlie,' he ses, 'what's the winner of the Durby?' I tells him and he ses to the Duke o' Lonsdale beside 'im, 'You should read Cheerful Charlie's chatter in this 'ere pink piper you should — I does every mornin' of my life after breakfast.' "'Charlie ye're a marvel,' he ses, and that's the reason why, when I've done you people a bit o' good — same as I done King George the Fifth, Gawd bless 'im, — I shall go 'ome, put my 'ead on my piller and sleep the sleep o' the just. 'Ere, 'oo wants the winner o' the Durby?"

☺   ☺   ☺

And the war of the sexes was in full flow back then:

"Husband and wife were watching the Derby field in the paddock.

"Suddenly one of the colts lashed out: 'How could such a beautiful thing have such a temper?' exclaimed the good lady.

"'Ah my dear,' replied the husband, 'I once thought the same about you.'"

☺   ☺   ☺

And staying with the ladies, here's another:

"One of the old school of trainers, having risen in the world, sent his daughter to a high-class ladies college.

"'She's a fine, well eddicated lass,' said he proudly to me one day. 'She don't call 'em 'osses like you an' me Willie — she calls them 'orses.'"

☺   ☺   ☺

If there's one thing which hasn't changed a great deal since the days when *Punter's Pie* was a new book, it is jockeys having to watch their weight:

"Before the invention of the Turkish and vapour bath, jockeys did their wasting by walking in heavy sweaters and by purging themselves with Epsom salts.

"When he lived in Worcestershire, Sam Darling of Isaac fame, great-grandfather of Sam and Fred of our day, once walked to Upton-on-Severn and knocked a chemist up for a dose of salts.

"After he had served him the chemist returned to the conjugal couch and his wife asked: 'How much have you got by being disturbed?'

"'About three pence, my dear.'

"'Fancy being disturbed for that amount.'

"'Never mind, my dear, Sam Darling will be much more disturbed than I have been before he reaches home.'"

☺   ☺   ☺

Here's one which might well hold good today:

"Once at Ayr a couple of would-be racegoers walked to

the officials gate saying, 'Starter and his assistant.'

"'But,' replied the gateman 'I've let the starter through.'

"'There's more than one race, yer fool,' was the instant retort. And their bluff succeeded too."

☺ ☺ ☺

Punter's Pie ran to 104 pages and there, on Page 104, ending the book, was the following yarn which presumably occupied that particular spot to close proceedings with a big laugh.

Did it succeed? Judge for yourself:

""Ow are yer getting on, 'Arry?' asked one racing camp follower of another at Gatwick.

"'Never touched a winner, Bob' was the reply.

"'Well, — is the trainer to foller 'ere, Arry.'

""Im? Why — 'e ain't saddled one in the first three yet, Bob.'

"'Naouw — but 'e as just dropped a quid note and I've picked it up — foller 'im, Arry.'"

☺ ☺ ☺

Even earlier than *Punter's Pie*, in 1925, a book titled, *Sporting and Dramatic Yarns*, compiled by RJB Sellar, devoted a whole chapter to racing and betting, calling it, 'They're Off.'

There follows a selection of its better tales:

Two racecourse crooks were standing chatting during a lull in business.

"Say, Bill," whispered one, "do you see that long bloke with the grey 'at and the telescopes slung rahn his waist?"

"Yus," said Bill.

"Well," continued the narrator of the story, "he must be

clean potty."

"How's that?" asked Bill.

"Why, 'is left 'and pocket is full o' tin-tacks."

☺   ☺   ☺

The sporting young man and his old-fashioned mother from the country were attending a race meeting; it was the old lady's first taste of the sport of kings.

"I say, mother," said the young man "I've been wondering for a long time what's in that bulky parcel you're carrying."

"Well," said the old lady "in your letter you said 'Bring something to put on the horses'.... So I brought this old eiderdown.... I hope it is not too shabby, my boy."

☺   ☺   ☺

The racing man was at the telephone.

"Hello, hello,' he bawled. "Can you tell me when the entries for the St Leger close?"

There came a startled gasp from the other end, and then a voice said: "But you must have got the wrong number; this is the Gas Company."

"Yes..yes...." said the sportsman imperturbably, "I know it's the Gas Company."

"Well, you must know that we don't know anything about the St Leger here," expostulated the official.

"Well, that's a pity," observed the sportsman. "You see, I wanted to enter our gas-meter."

☺   ☺   ☺

The 3.30 had just come to an exciting finish with the favourite nowhere.

"I say," growled one disappointed punter turning to his friend at the rails. "I thought you told me that Barrackroom Boy was a foregone conclusion for this race?"

His friend's face was flushed with wrath and disappointment: "Well, he WAS the conclusion, wasn't he?" he growled.

☺   ☺   ☺

Two racing men were deep-sea fishing. So strongly was the gambling instinct implanted in them that, before they had dropped their lines into the ocean, there was a ten-shilling bet made over the first catch.

A few minutes later, with a whoop of triumph, one of them pulled up a struggling flatfish.

The other immediately produced half a crown. "Look here," said the lucky fisher indignantly, "our bet was half a quid, not half a dollar."

"I know that, old man," smirked the other "but you only get quarter odds for a plaice, you know."

☺   ☺   ☺

The jockeys were weighing in before an important race.

"Good heavens, William," groaned a distracted owner, "you are getting heavier. Can't you take something of?"

"No, sir," whined the long-suffering knight of the pigskin. "I'm wearing me lightest clothes.... I haven't tasted a morsel of food or drink today, and I've just cut my finger-nails."

The owner consulted his watch. "Look here," he said swiftly "there's just time to nip out and get a shave."

☺   ☺   ☺

A Scotsman attended a race meeting for the first time in his life and, after a few events had been run, his friends persuaded him to put a shilling on a horse.

Very reluctantly, and without conviction, he tendered the coin to the bookmaker and awaited the result of the race.

To his amazement, the horse won at 10 to 1, and he dashed to collect his winnings.

The bookie paid him eleven single shillings, and the Scot bit each one carefully.

"Wot's up?" demanded the bookie indignantly. "D'ye fink my money ain't good?"

"Na, na, ma mannie," responded the Scotsman cautiously "but I just wanted to mak' sure that the shillin' I gave ye wasna amang them."

The farmer's son was the worst dunce in school. "Dear me," wailed the much-tried teacher, "surely YOU ought to know what a harness is? You've lived all your life on a farm and you don't know that. Now think boy. What is it your father puts on the horses every day?"

The rustic youth grinned with sudden cunning: "I know what tha be drivin' at now, miss.... He puts on 'arf a crown each way, does faather."

It was the dreaded day of the oral history examination.

The teacher had fired off a few quick questions to the wilting class, and then Smith Minor's turn came.

"Now then, Smith," rasped the teacher "give me the various races that have dominated England since the days of the Romans."

Smith fidgeted nervously for a moment, then he gulped: "The Derby.... Cesarewitch, Lincolnshire, Grand National and Oaks, sir."

With blanched face and trembling fingers, Mrs Brown took the telegram into her husband in the study.

"John," she said in tremulous accents "here's a wire from Jack to say he's been injured at Kempton Park races."

"Oh dear, isn't it terrible?"

Mr Brown seized the telegram and scanned it carefully.

"Selfish young cub," he muttered. "He always thinks of himself. Why, he doesn't give the winner of the 2.30."

☺ ☺ ☺

The punter had had a bad day.

In an attempt to retrieve some of his losses, he put his last bean on an outsider in the final race, and to his intense joy it romped home at twenty to one.

To the backer's chagrin, however, he found, when he went to collect his winnings, that the bookmaker had romped home at twenty five to five.

☺ ☺ ☺

"Get up you lazy thing," cried the wife of the somnolent punter, "it's twenty to one."

"Right-o my dear," came the sleepy reply. "Put on a quid each way for me."

☺ ☺ ☺

In their more expansive moments, bookmakers occasionally condescend to discuss the little ways of their friends the punters.

Anyhow, two of the fraternity were engaged on the agreeable topic at their club.

Said one: "I had a curious experience once. Lord B— keeps an account with me, you know, and on one occasion he settled up the same account twice."

"Really?" said the other "that WAS remarkable. What did you do?"

"Well," confessed the first bookie "I was a bit flummoxed

to know what to do, but at last I came to what I think was
the only solution."

"Yes, what was it?"

"I rendered the account again."

☺   ☺   ☺

An American had been entertaining a little sporting gathering with stories of some close finishes he had
witnessed, and incidentally cited the classical instance of
the yacht which had secured the verdict over its rival by a
mere coat of paint.

Feeling that the honour of Britain was at stake, a grizzled
old sportsman who had followed the Turf for many years
took up the challenge,

"I remember down at Ascot one year," he said reminis-
cently "two horses ran neck and neck from the starting
gate to within a hundred yards of the finish.

"At that point a wasp stung one of the gees on the nose.
Gentlemen, that race was won by a blister."

☺   ☺   ☺

A benevolent old gentleman saw a shabbily dressed man
at the corner of a street, and the sight aroused his pity.

"What a shame that the old fellow should have to beg,"
murmured the philanthropist, fishing for a shilling.

He approached the seedy one, and murmuring, "Never
say die," gave him the coin and trotted off, conscious of
having done his day's good deed.

Later in the day, as he was passing the same corner, the
shabby lounger thrust a Treasury note in the old gentleman's hand and hoarsely whispered: "Won at 20 to 1, sir."

☺   ☺   ☺

"Hello, Hunt," said Blunt, as he encountered his old friend

on the street. "You are the very man I want to meet. Our office is organising a sweepstake on the big race tomorrow, and I feel sure that you will take a five-bob ticket."

"Certainly I shall, old man," said Hunt with alacrity. "But as it happens I don't have five shillings at the moment."

"Oh, that's all right," said Blunt, "I shall be seeing you tomorrow in any case to give you the result of the sweep, and you can pay then."

Next day when the friends met again, Blunt wore an expansive smile.

"What do you think, my dear fellow?" he chortled, "I won the first prize in the sweep yesterday. Wasn't I lucky?"

"What about the second prize?" inquired Hunt hopefully.

"As a matter of fact my younger brother won that," explained Blunt. "Wasn't he lucky?"

"He certainly was," muttered Hunt darkly. "And who won the third prize?"

"Oh, my kid sister won that," said Blunt "Wasn't she lucky? And, er, you didn't pay me for your ticket, Hunt."

"I know," said Hunt, as he moved away, "Wasn't I lucky?"

☺ ☺ ☺

Pat was travelling home on a race train. He had not been to the races and knew nothing about the Turf, so a friendly bookmaker undertook to explain things.

"You see," said the bookie "if you back a horse for a bob and it comes in at ten to one you win ten bob.

"Similarly, if you back it at five to one you're five bob to the good. Do you understand that?"

"Sure I do that," said Pat promptly. "But I'm not quite clear about what happens if the beast comes in at one o'clock."

☺ ☺ ☺

He was having one of those rare 'days off from the missus' and, of course, he went to the races. He knew little enough about racing but he bought a card and glanced down the list of entries for the first race and decided to venture a pound on 'Behave Yourself'.

To everybody's astonishment the horse won at 20/1.

"How in the world did you manage to pick him out?" asked a disgruntled punter who had lost badly on the race.

The lucky fellow smiled. "I'm a believer in omens," he said with a chuckle "and the last thing my wife said before I left this morning was 'Behave yourself'."

☺   ☺   ☺

Two unlucky punters were returning from the races.

A fair was in progress in the racecourse grounds, and the two luckless ones stopped to gaze at the cheerfully whirling steeds of the merry-go-rounds.

"What a change it is," one of them murmured 'to see form working out dead correct every time."

☺   ☺   ☺

He had returned from the steeplechase meeting very depressed.

He had not succeeded in finding a single winner all day.

His wife heard his tale of woe in surprise not unmixed with indignation.

"It's a peculiar thing you always win at cards," she said coldly. "Why can't you win at the races as well?"

"Ah," replied the sportsman moodily "you see, they don't let me shuffle the horses."

☺   ☺   ☺

He was the kind of man who is known as 'the bookies friend'. That is to say, he was a sportsman and an optimist, chiefly the latter, but his friends generally had a flutter on the numerous 'good things' he gave away.

After a big race one day one of his disconsolate victims approached him. "I say," he protested "you fairly did me down over the 3.30.... after saying I could put my shirt on it, too."

"Never mind," consoled the chronic optimist, "just think what you'll save on next week's laundry."

☺   ☺   ☺

A man in a state of great agitation rushed into the 'silver ring' at a big race meeting.

"Hats off, hats off," he shouted, and the somewhat surprised spectators automatically obeyed him. "What's up?" inquired one of the hatless punters. "Is the King coming?"

"Not as far as I know," answered the agitated one "but I've just been welched by a bald-headed bookie."

☺   ☺   ☺

A gentleman from the North went to a race meeting with a party of friends, but he abstained from betting until several members of the party had won considerable sums.

Then, after much agitated heart-searchings, Jock laid five shillings on a horse which, later, romped home at 20/1.

As the bookie nonchalantly paid out the winnings in Treasury notes the Scot gasped hoarsely: "Tell me, ma man, how lang has this sort o' thing been goin' on?"

ODDS & SODS

Ticklish allsorts

Brough Scott recalled a 1985 conversation with Lord Cadogan of the Jockey Club, during which the noble Lord, evidently believing it to be a compliment, told Scott: "I think things have moved a long way. I mean my grand-father would never have dreamt of talking to someone like you."

☺   ☺   ☺

The rural vicar was requested to offer up prayers for Lucy Gray at his next service on Sunday, which he duly did.
Later in the week he was told by the same parishioner that it would not be necessary to repeat the supplications on the next Sunday.
"Is Miss Gray now fully recovered?" asked the vicar.
"Recovered? She won at 6/1 on Tuesday — didn't you back her? Everyone else in the village did."

☺   ☺   ☺

Then there was the keen racegoing burglar who broke into the betting shop to steal the safe and while he was there lost £500.

☺   ☺   ☺

Famous diarist and owner of 1837 St Leger winner Mango, Charles Greville, wrote in 1838: "Racing is just like dram drinking; momentary excitement and wretched intervals; full consciousness of the mischievous effects of the habit and equal difficulty in abstaining from it."

☺   ☺   ☺

Father and son returned after their day out together.
"And how did you enjoy the zoo, Johnny?" asked Mum.
"It was great," said Johnny "especially when one of the animals came racing home at 20/1."

☺   ☺   ☺

They do say that a racehorse is the only animal capable of taking thousands of people for a ride at the same time.

☺   ☺   ☺

Then there was the steeplechaser nicknamed Niagara — because of his continuous falls.

☺   ☺   ☺

In horse racing there is nothing so uncertain as a certainty.

☺   ☺   ☺

A man walking along the road on his way to the races saw a horse looking over a hedge.
As he passed by the horse it said to him: "Do you know, I won the Grand National twelve years ago?"
The man was so amazed that he rushed straight into the nearby pub and ordered a large scotch, telling the barman that he'd just had a nasty shock.
"Don't tell me, that horse out there has been talking to you?" said the barman.
"Yes," replied the man.

"What did he say to you?" asked the barman.

"He told me he won the National twelve years ago."

"Hmm, bloody typical. He's a compulsive liar, he was only second."

☺   ☺   ☺

The new Steward was out with a more experienced colleague watching a race.

As the horses finished the race they both noticed one being tenderly ridden along at the back of the field, the jockey obviously not making any serious attempt to win.

"Did you see that?" asked the new Steward.

"Hmm, yes indeed," replied his colleague.

"And what do you think we should do about it?"

"Well, I think we should back it next time out, don't you?"

☺   ☺   ☺

Three racehorses walked into a public bar together, ordered three pints and stood chatting. One of them asked his two mates if they had been racing recently.

"Yes," replied the grey horse, "I ran at Doncaster on Saturday and, do you know, I was ten lengths behind the leader with two furlongs to go when I felt a ruddy great needle stuck in my behind — well, I nearly took off. I've never moved so fast. Anyway, I won by a neck at 14/1."

"Well, I never," said the black horse. "I ran at Pontefract three weeks ago and I was tailed off with half a mile to go when I felt a needle in my rump — boy, did I shift. My jockey could hardly pull me up after the race. I won by three lengths at 20/1."

"Funny you should both tell me that," said the third horse, a chestnut, "because I wondered whether that had happened to you, too. When I was running in a hurdle

race at Catterick on Friday I felt a needle in my behind —
well, after that I could have jumped Becher's Brook. I won
by ten lengths at 12/1."

Just then, a greyhound sitting in the corner with his pint
interrupted their conversation.

"Excuse me," he said "I couldn't help but hear your
conversation. I ran at Wimbledon last Tuesday and at the
second bend I was well behind when all of a sudden
someone chucked something at me from the crowd. I felt
this needle go into my rear end and I flew round the last
two bends and won by a short head."

"Well, would you believe it?" said the grey, the black and
the chestnut racehorses in unison — "A bloody talking
greyhound."

☺   ☺   ☺

Punters and betting-shop staff watched in astonishment
as a scruffy-looking individual walked through the door
waving his arms about and calling to someone outside:
"That's it, gently does it, bring her in now."

As he continued to call and wave, the rear quarters of a
horse appeared in the doorway, followed slowly by the
back of the horse and then, finally, its head.

"What the bloody hell do you think you're doing?" yelled
the shop manager at the scruffy individual who looked at
him calmly and said: "Oh, I didn't think you'd mind — the
bloke outside said anyone could back a horse in here."

☺   ☺   ☺

The night before the Grand National a young couple were
discovered on the course making love by Becher's Brook.
They were arrested for offending public decency and
appeared in court the next morning — when they asked

for ten other fences to be taken into consideration.

☺   ☺   ☺

A ventriloquist on holiday in Newmarket came across a large stud farm.

He asked for a tour of the place and was escorted around by one of the stable lads.

As he was shown the highly valuable stallions and their partners the ventriloquist began to make the horses 'talk'. Startled, the lad raced off to tell his boss what was happening, shouting: "Them 'orses be talkin' — but if any of they mares be sayin' anythin' about me then they be lyin'."

☺   ☺   ☺

A jockeys' team were playing the local cricket side in a match, but they were one player short until a local trainer offered them the services of one of his horses.

"Can he bowl?" asked the jockeys' skipper, doubtfully.

"Of course, just stick the ball in his hoof," said the trainer. They put him on to bowl and were astonished as he proceeded to take six wickets.

"Can he bat?" asked the jockeys' skipper.

"Of course — just put the bat between his front hooves."

In went the padded-up horse to open the batting. He hit the first ball firmly towards the boundary.

"Run," shouted the jockeys' skipper, beginning to advance down the wicket.

"Run?" said the trainer, "don't be stupid — if he could bloody well run I'd have entered him for the Derby."

☺   ☺   ☺

A woman spotted her racing fanatic husband poring over the racing pages of the newspaper: "I don't know why you're wasting your time trying to find the winners — they'll all be listed in the *Sporting Life* tomorrow."

☺   ☺   ☺

The stable lad was new at the game and when the local steward at the racecourse asked him about his horse's pedigree he was lost for words.

"What do you mean by pedigree exactly?"

"I mean — what is he by and what is he out of?"

"Well, he's by himself and he's outside the stable door."

☺   ☺   ☺

The police watched the horse box come hammering down the country road at least thirty miles faster than the speed limit.

They chased after it and made it pull over, got out and walked over to the driver.

"Where are you off to in such a hurry, sir?"

"I have to get to the races — I'm the travelling head lad for one of the biggest stables in Newmarket."

The policemen walked around to the back of the horse box to take a look inside.

It was empty. "There are no horses in your horse box, sir."

"No, of course there aren't — I'm taking the non-runners."

☺   ☺   ☺

The keen racegoer was off on a round-the-world trip.

In Switzerland he entered a raffle in a bar and won himself a multi-lingual parrot which, like most Swiss, could speak several languages.

Realising the gambling potential of his new pet the race-goer quickly flew back to London and set off for the races, along with the parrot.

Arriving at Newbury he made his way to the racecourse

bar where he he placed his parrot on the counter and offered to bet fellow racegoers that his bird could converse in English, German or French.

The bet was quickly taken and the gambler asked the parrot: "Sprechen sie Deutsch?"

Silence. Not a peep. Nary a squawk.

The punter, now in a seriously bad mood, paid his debts and took his parrot away. When he got home he told the parrot: "I've a good mind to strangle you — you let me down badly."

"Don't be stupid," said the parrot "think of the odds you'll get tomorrow."

☺   ☺   ☺

As Brough Scott was once heard to remark during a race commentary: "And there's the unmistakable figure of Joe Mercer — or is it Lester Piggott?"

☺   ☺   ☺

Following a race with a close finish, David Coleman told TV viewers: "And that's the magic of television, I've just been told over the headphones who finished third."

☺   ☺   ☺

"These two horses have met on five occasions this season, and I think they've beaten each other on each occasion." Somewhat bemusing observation in pre-race comments by Jimmy Lindley.

☺   ☺   ☺

Whilst strolling along to the racecourse, dreaming of backing a few winners and making a bob or two, the racing man was startled out of his pleasant daydream when he came across an ugly, wizened, gargoyle-like dwarf.

The bizarre creature accosted the racegoer, saying in a high pitched, reedy voice: "I'm the punter's friend, the Magic Pixie — I can make all your dreams come true and grant you three wishes."

"Wonderful!" gasped the racegoer. "Let me think — well, I'd like to go through the card this afternoon, then I'd like to become a racehorse owner, then I'd like my horse to win the Derby so that I could make a fortune by putting him at stud."

"Fine, no problem," said the Magic Pixie. "And all it takes for you to be granted your three wishes is for you to make love to me."

"What?" demanded the racegoer, "you must be joking."

"Please yourself," said the Pixie "but you'll never get another opportunity like this."

Steeling himself for the ordeal, the punter finally realised that this could be his big chance of making a fortune, so he ushered the Pixie into a shadowy corner of a nearby field and did the distasteful job.

Afterwards, the punter got up, brushed himself down and said: "Right, and now for my three wishes," to the Magic Pixie, who was just lighting up a cigarette and looking very happy with the world.

Smiling contentedly, the Magic Pixie asked the racegoer: "How old are you?"

"How old? What's that got to do with anything — I'm 45."

"Forty five?" said the Pixie "forty five. And you STILL believe in Magic Pixies?"

As television commentator, Julian Wilson, was heard to remark in April 1992: "When you've got a good filly underneath you, problems tend to evaporate."

☺   ☺   ☺

Then there was the gambling mad vet who crossed a racehorse with a giraffe to get a runner which would never be beaten in a photo finish.

☺   ☺   ☺

As the Tortoise, the unbacked outsider, came to the finish line a long-odds winner of the big race with the heavily backed Hare, he was met by race officials who had warned bookmakers to withhold payment pending the result of their enquiries and drug tests.

☺   ☺   ☺

When rugby league player, Ricky Cowan, was looking for a new club in June 1993, a friend volunteered to circulate his details to possibly interested Clubs.

But he was a little surprised to receive a reply from Doncaster asking: "How is he over seven furlongs."

It turned out he'd faxed the racecourse instead of the rugby club!

☺   ☺   ☺

Two friends were discussing a weighty problem — one of them was considerably overweight and was wondering what he could do about this situation.

"Why not go racing?" suggested the other. "Walk to the track, run down to look at the horses in the paddock, sprint to the bookies to back one of them, rush over to watch the race then dash back to collect your winnings.

"After a few days you'll soon start to shed weight."

The chubby chap decided to act on this advice and duly became a regular at the track.

A couple of weeks later the pals met up again. "Well," said the friend "I'm not sure whether you've lost any weight or not, how have you been getting on?"

Replied the portly punter: "I went to the course and had just dashed down to the paddock when a stable lad threw a saddle on me by mistake."

"No!" said the friend "surely not — so what did you do?"

"What COULD I do? I gave my jockey a superb ride and finished third at 20/1."

☺   ☺   ☺

A man's past is known as history; a woman's history is known as her past, but a horse's past is known as form.

☺   ☺   ☺

From the magazine *Inside Racing* comes this story of the late racing journalist Jim Stanford of the *Daily Mail.*

Following a press trip to Sheikh Mohammed's Dalham Hall Stud at which the booze had flowed freely for the hacks, Jim was trying to exit via automatic glass doors.

"But due to the effects of his host's generosity he couldn't quite work out which pane of glass he should be aiming for.

"Fellow hacks looked on nearly in tears as poor Jim kept bouncing back off the glass walls.

"Finally, he turned round and addressed the assembled gathering. 'Bloody hell,' he exclaimed. 'If these Arabs are this effing rich you'd think they could afford door handles.'"

☺   ☺   ☺

"Sorry we didn't have time for the Memory Lane feature," said presenter Derek Thompson to *Morning Line* viewers in March 1993. "But we'll show you that in the future."

☺   ☺   ☺

The ex-jockey opened up a pub-restaurant and stocked it with memorabilia from his career, including a number of bronzes of well known horses.

One night a customer was asking about the bronzes.

"That one over there was my great grand-father's first winner — the one next to it was my grandfather's first winner, at the side of that one is my Dad's first winner and next to that one, my own first winner."

"And that one over there — which is that?" asked the customer.

"We never talk about that one, it put my Mum in hospital."

"Oh, did she ride as well?"

"No," said the ex-jockey "she was sitting there last Saturday night having a half of lager and it fell on her."

☺   ☺   ☺

Amongst horse names which have given commentators problems over the years, Wear The Fox Hat, Shy Talk and the American runner Honk A Wanker, figure near the top of the list.

☺   ☺   ☺

Two horses were on their way to the start.

As they reached the stalls and slowed down one turned to the other and said, "Excuse me, I can't remember your mane — but your pace is familiar."

☺   ☺   ☺

Actor, gambler and racing fanatic Robert Morley died at the age of 84 on Derby day, 1992. Paying tribute to him on TV, commentator Brough Scott issued his sympathies — to Mr Morley's parents.

☺ ☺ ☺

The beautiful young girl went into the library and asked the librarian: "Can you recommend something I'll enjoy?"
Asked the librarian, 'Do you like Dick Francis?'
"O' Of course I do" she replied, "But my name isn't Frances."

☺ ☺ ☺

Then there was the female racehorse who kept all her engagements and appointments neatly jotted down in her Filly-o-Fax.

☺ ☺ ☺

The sign outside the Newmarket church read: "What would you do if Jesus returned amongst you tomorrow?" Underneath was scrawled, 'Jock Piggott off the favourite.'

☺ ☺ ☺

The Underwater Derby was about tocome under orders — betting was fast and furious, with the big money goinmg on 6/4 favourite The Speedy Crab, with 5/2 offered about Jumping Jellfish and 6/11 Shady Shrimp.
Honest Octopus, the sub-marine bookie was doing a roaring trade and as the starter prepared to send the field on its way up rushed Danny Dolphin, desperate to get his bet on — "Listen" he said to Honest Octopus, "I've had a tip for one, here, I want 6 pounds on Jumping Jellfish, but I've come out without my wallet, will you take the bet and I'll pay you later if I lose."
"Well, okay" said Honest Octopus, handing over a ticket for six pounds to win on Jumping Jellyfish.
Off went the race and in a thriling finish The Speedy Crab just beat the fast finishing Jumping Jellyfish.
After settling up with the winning punters Honest Octopus

looked around for Danny Dolphin who was nowhere to be seen.

"Damn, looks like he's done a runner with my six pounds" he thought.

Several days passed and the Octopus was beginning to doubt whether he would ever be paid when he spotted Danny swimming towards him together with a rather aneamic looking companion, Sonny Squid.

"Oh, there you are at last" Honest Octopus greeted Danny Dolphin. "Your mate doesn't look too well, does he? I take it you've come to settle up?"

"Yes" said Danny, pushing the ill-looking Sonny towards Honest Octopus. "There you are."

"What do you mean?" asked Honest.

"Well" said Danny, "That's the sick squid I owe you."

☺   ☺   ☺

"The form book should be written in braille for the benefit of the stewards," said racing journalist, the late Clive Graham.

☺   ☺   ☺

"Experience of racing, though desirable, is not essential." ......1980 Jockey Club advertisement for stipendiary stewards.

☺   ☺   ☺

A very smart lady named Cookie
Said "I like to mix gambling with nookie.
Before every race
I go home to my place
And curl up with a very good bookie."

☺   ☺   ☺

"Dear Bastard. You could not tip more rubbish if London Weekend bought you a fork-lift truck."

......Fan letter to Lord Oaksey.

☺   ☺   ☺

Turf raconteur and punter Jeffrey Bernard told of the time "I fancied a horse with a strange Arab name that was running at Newmarket and a woman kindly volunteered to walk to the betting shop and back it for me. When she came back with the slip I saw that she had backed the wrong horse and not my selection. I wasn't best pleased.

"We watched the race on television and I was about to swear at her and call her a silly cow when her wrong horse hit the front and went away to win rather easily at 6/1.

"She was so daft she even thanked me for the tip, having backed it herself."

☺   ☺   ☺

A wealthy artist decided to build up a stud of racehorses, and he commissioned a sporting friend to make the purchases.

But his friend was no particular judge of horse-flesh, and when the artist arrived at the stable one day to inspect the new arrivals he was confronted by a scraggy bunch of sorry-looking hacks.

"Good Lord," exclaimed the prospective owner, "what are these?"

"Your horses," said his friend in aggrieved accents.

"Rub them out and do them over again," groaned the artist.

☺   ☺   ☺

The proprietor of a restaurant heard reports from several

of his customers that his waiters were very slack, and much more inclined to discuss the day's racing than attend to orders.

Determined to find out if these allegations were true, he kept his eyes and ears open.

On the day of a big race he heard one of the waiters shout down the hoist: "Poached egg, one," and to the proprietor's horror a hoarse and agitated voice asked from the lower regions: "What was second and third, mate?"

OTHER TITLES
From Pride Of Place

Send your order to:
Pride Of Place (UK)
PO Box 70, Chorley, Lancashire PR6 7SB
(£2.00 p & p needs to be added to each order)

Sporting Skulduggery
By Graham Sharpe

By the author of Horse Laughs, an hilarious review of the crafty, cunning and cheating ploys adopted to win at sport. The unethical, devious and shameless are all wittily chronicled in this book which is as fast moving as the sporting rascals it portrays.
Paperback £4.99

The Coup
by Ken Payne

A true life roller-coaster ride of wild gambling, sex and scandal that rocked the racing world. The Coup is a no-holds barred autobiography, a romp of a read, and a shocking expose about the use of drugs in racing.
Paperback £4.99

The Boss
by Charles Lambert

A rivetting and revealing account of the stresses and strains, passion and pressure, agony and ecstasy that football managers in the 1990s have to come to terms with. In The Boss, top managers tell it how it really is living on the razor's edge in Britain's national game.
Hardback £14.99

GAMBLING

Always Back Winners

By Stewart Simpson

The most sought after horse racing system ever published! Reprinted for a third tim in just 12 months. The book reveals how a former Clydeside shipyard worker made a fortune gambling. Priceless information on the author's unique, successful 'system'.
Paperback £9.99

The Golf Form Book 1996

by Keith Elliott

The definitive guide to successful golf betting. The 1995 annual, universally acclaimed in the sporting press, was a best-selling smash hit and tipped tournament winners at 80/1, 66/1, 50/1 and 25 others at prices as high as 40/1.
Paperback £14.99

Two Year Olds of 1995

by Steve Taplin

The punter's ultimate winner finding weapon for this year - and next! Now in its 11th edition, the book has uncovered five of the last nine Derby winners, before they had even made a telling hoofprint on the racecourse. The 'Classic' book choice for punters who want to show a profit from betting.
Paperback £4.99

RACING

A Long Time Gone

By Chris Pitt

An enthralling and nostalgic account of EVERY racecourse in the UK that has closed in the 20th century. The book vividly recreates a 'lost' rustic world of sporting heroes who graced the Sport of Kings and Queens.
Hardback £24.99

Fit For A Queen

by Richard Pitman

A compelling portrait of the Queen Mother's 50 year fascination with horseracing. The book brilliantly captures an insider's view of the glory, drama, fun and passion the Queen Mum has enjoyed and experienced in the sport.
Hardback £17.99

From Rags to Riches

by John Budden

Everyone wants a bargain, everyone loves a champion - this book tells the engaging story of 16 racehorses that have been both! From Rags To Riches details evocatively how equine stars such as Lochsong, Jodami, Mister Baileys and Flakey Dove defied the odds to make it to become racing legends.
Paperback £7.99

FOOTBALL

Back Where We Belong
By Eddie Cotton

A frank and intimate diary of Liverpool's renaissance and return to Europe under Roy Evans. The book is a behind-the-scenes exposé of how this great football club functions during the trials, tribulations and triumphs of a ten month season.
Paperback £4.99

Scouting For Glory
by Fred O'Donoghue

The first book which pulls back the wraps on the rarely revealed twilight world of football scouts. Written by a man with a lifetime's experience in the job, the book dispenses invaluable advice and guidance to youngsters who want to embark on a career as a professional footballer.
Paperback £9.99

In a League of their Own!
by Gail Newsham

The spellbinding story of the pioneers of women's soccer, Dick, Kerr Ladies Football Club.
1/2 price hardback £4.99 *(rrp £14.99)*